Devil's Advocates

DEVIL'S ADVOCATES is a series of books devoted to exploring the classics of horror cinema. Contributors to the series come from the fields of teaching, academia, journalism and fiction, but all have one thing in common: a passion for the horror film and a desire to share it with the widest possible audience.

'The admirable Devil's Advocates series is not only essential – and fun – reading for the serious horror fan but should be set texts on any genre course.'
Dr Ian Hunter, Reader in Film Studies, De Montfort University, Leicester

'Auteur Publishing's new Devil's Advocates critiques on individual titles... offer bracingly fresh perspectives from passionate writers. The series will perfectly complement the BFI archive volumes.' **Christopher Fowler,** *Independent on Sunday*

'Devil's Advocates has proven itself more than capable of producing impassioned, intelligent analyses of genre cinema... quickly becoming the go-to guys for intelligent, easily digestible film criticism.' *HorrorTalk.com*

'Auteur Publishing continue the good work of giving serious critical attention to significant horror films.' *Black Static*

facebook DevilsAdvocatesbooks

DevilsAdBooks

Also available in this series

A Girl Walks Home Alone at Night Farshid Kazemi
Black Sunday Martyn Conterio
The Blair Witch Project Peter Turner
Blood and Black Lace Roberto Curti
The Blood on Satan's Claw David Evans-Powell
The Cabin in the Woods Susanne Kord
Candyman Jon Towlson
Cannibal Holocaust Calum Waddell
Cape Fear Rob Daniel
Carrie Neil Mitchell
The Company of Wolves James Gracey
The Conjuring Kevin J. Wetmore Jr.
The Craft Miranda Corcoran
Creepshow Simon Brown
Cruising Eugenio Ercolani & Marcus Stiglegger
The Curse of Frankenstein Marcus K. Harmes
Daughters of Darkness Kat Ellinger
Dawn of the Dead Jon Towlson
Dead of Night Jez Conolly & David Bates
The Descent James Marriot
The Devils Darren Arnold
Don't Look Now Jessica Gildersleeve
The Evil Dead Lloyd Haynes
The Fly Emma Westwood
Frenzy Ian Cooper
Halloween Murray Leeder
House of Usher Evert Jan van Leeuwen
In the Mouth of Madness Michael Blyth
IT: Chapters 1 & 2 Alissa Burger
It Follows Joshua Grimm
Ju-on The Grudge Marisa Hayes
Let the Right One In Anne Billson
M Samm Deighan
Macbeth Rebekah Owens
The Mummy Doris V. Sutherland
Nosferatu Cristina Massaccesi
The Omen Adrian Schober
Peeping Tom Kiri Bloom Walden
Pet Sematary Shellie McMurdo
Poltergeist Rob McLaughlin
Possession Alison Taylor
Prevenge Andrew Graves
Re-Animator Eddie Falvey
Repulsion Jeremy Carr
Saw Benjamin Poole
Scream Steven West
The Shining Laura Mee
Shivers Luke Aspell
The Silence of the Lambs Barry Forshaw
Snuff Mark McKenna
Suspiria Alexandra Heller-Nicholas
The Texas Chain Saw Massacre James Rose
The Thing Jez Conolly
Trouble Every Day Kate Robertson
Twin Peaks: Fire Walk With Me Lindsay Hallam
The Witch Brandon Grafius
The Wicker Man Steve A. Wiggins
Witchfinder General Ian Cooper

Devil's Advocates

I Walked with a Zombie

Clive Dawson

Acknowledgements

I'd like to extend my sincere gratitude to John Atkinson at Auteur for giving me the opportunity to write this volume. Huge thanks, also, to my wife Shirley, my daughter Sherilyn and my sister and her husband, Janet and Trevor Wakefield, for their love and support. Special thanks must go to five people who have been particularly supportive, listed in alphabetical order: Harald Gruenberger, Steve Haberman, Gregory Mank, Stefani Warren and Tom Weaver. The help and kindness of many others also made this book possible: Allan Bryce, David Colton, Alan Hornsey, Richard Keenan, Michael Lee, Constantine Nasr, Michael Price, Laurence Rubin, Amy Schireson and Peggy Ueda. I'm extremely grateful to the staff of the following institutions: Kristine Krueger and Genevieve Maxwell at the Margaret Herrick Library, Neil Hodge and Molly Haigh at UCLA, Ned Comstock at USC, Amy Reytar at the US National Archives, Cristina Meisner at the Harry Ransom Centre of the University of Texas, Frank Bowles at Cambridge University Library, Ann Sindelar at the Western Reserve Historical Society, plus all the staff at the BFI Reuben Library and Special Collections, the British Library and the Cleveland Public Library. Finally, I must single out for particular praise three people who helped immeasurably with my research: Brook Darnell, Andre Solnikkar and Karina Wilson.

First published in 2023 by
Auteur, an imprint of
Liverpool University Press,
4 Cambridge Street,
Liverpool
L69 7ZU

Series design: Nikki Hamlett at Cassels Design
Set by Cassels Design, Luton UK
Printed and bound by CPI Group (UK) Ltd, Croydon CR0 4YY

All rights reserved. No part of this publication may be reproduced in any material form (including photocopying or storing in any medium by electronic means and whether or not transiently or incidentally to some other use of this publication) without the permission of the copyright owner.

British Library Cataloguing-in-Publication Data
A catalogue record for this book is available from the British Library

ISBN hardback: 9781837645169
eISBN: 9781837644902

Contents

Introduction 1

Chapter 1: The Snake Pit 3

Chapter 2: 'Jane Eyre in the West Indies' 13

Chapter 3: I Walked with a Zombie 39

Chapter 4: 'Most Smashing Sleeper of the Season' 89

Chapter 5: Legacy 105

Bibliography 115

INTRODUCTION

In 1942, Hollywood producer Val Lewton led a modest revolution, initiating a series of films for RKO Radio Pictures that broke the hegemony Universal Pictures had effectively held over screen horror since the early 1930s whilst radically redefining the genre. The exact nature of his groundbreaking approach is examined in this volume. Widely regarded as a *producer auteur*, Lewton completed eleven films at RKO and the influence of this seminal body of work on 1940s cinema and beyond is still being explored today, particularly in the context of the rich cross-fertilisation of genres that took place during that decade.

Lewton's cycle began with the phenomenally successful *Cat People* (1942). His second film, *I Walked with a Zombie* (1943) – about a Canadian nurse who accepts a job on the Caribbean island of St Sebastian to care for a woman who may or may not be the victim of voodoo – pushed the boundaries of screen narrative even further. Completed before *Cat People* had even been released, the film was an audacious throw of the dice for a new B-movie producer who'd not yet proven his worth to a studio hovering on the verge of bankruptcy and desperate for a turnaround in its box-office fortunes. *Cat People*'s success might have been regarded as a one-off had *Zombie*'s critical reception and box-office draw not proven its equal, cementing the reputation of both Lewton and director Jacques Tourneur.

Despite the lurid, studio-imposed title, *Zombie* is a subtle and ambiguous visual poem loosely inspired by Charlotte Brontë's *Jane Eyre* and Daphne du Maurier's *Rebecca*. It also advanced a daring condemnation of slavery and colonialism at a time when such themes were being suppressed by the Office of War Information, simultaneously breaking new ground in the representation of black people on screen.

The first part of this volume charts the complex development and production of the project – essential to understanding the concerns and intentions of the filmmakers in the context of wartime Hollywood – based on extensive primary research that uncovered a wealth of new material. The central portion of the book consists of a detailed analysis of the film, referencing a broad range of historical and academic studies of the audio-visual text. The final section explores the film's reception and the influence this and other Lewton productions exerted on genre cinema.

DEVIL'S ADVOCATES

I'm hopeful that this monograph will lead to a more widespread appreciation of a unique genre classic, described in *Robin Wood on the Horror Film* as 'perhaps the most delicate poetic fantasy in the American cinema'.

Chapter 1: The Snake Pit

To fully appreciate the context in which *I Walked with a Zombie* was developed and produced, it's first necessary to understand how Val Lewton's RKO production unit came into being, the foundations of his new approach to screen horror, and something of the character of Lewton himself.

Russian émigré Lewton, born in Yalta in 1904, was brought to the USA as a young child after his mother Nina left her husband to join her sister, the stage and screen star Alla Nazimova, in New York. Consequently, two strong, independent women raised him, without the influence of a father figure. An avid reader with a vivid imagination he was, by all accounts, difficult to handle. As an adult, his pre-RKO career consisted of three main phases: he learned the craft of writing during stints as a journalist and freelance author of poetry, short stories and novels; the business of film promotion working in the publicity department at MGM in New York; and finally, the art of filmmaking as the story editor to legendary producer David O. Selznick in Hollywood. Here, he was intimately involved with the development of such classics as *A Tale of Two Cities* (1935) – for which he arranged the revolutionary battle scenes in conjunction with second-unit director Jacques Tourneur – *Gone with the Wind* (1939), *Rebecca* (1940) and *Jane Eyre* (1944).[1] He was a complex character – a 'huge, burly, kindly man with a quick sense of humor and pleasant and courteous manners', according to *Cat People* writer DeWitt Bodeen. Yet he was also extremely insecure. He 'loathed physical contact on a social basis' and was also 'extremely shy, and easily hurt if his superiors failed to go along with him on story and production plans, for he was remarkably honest and well-disciplined, and accepted only the best'.[2]

RKO BECKONS

In April 1941, the newly installed general manager at RKO, Joseph Breen, asked Lewton whether he'd be interested in the position of 'super-story-editor' at the studio. Breen had run the industry censorship body, the Production Code Administration (PCA), for seven years, knew Lewton from his work for Selznick, and considered him the 'best story man in Hollywood'.[3] Lewton, despite his loyalty to Selznick and the financial security that his position provided, had long been eager to explore new opportunities. However, Breen's position at RKO soon became insecure and the proposed job never materialised. Nevertheless, before his eventual return to the PCA Breen recommended Lewton to Charles Koerner, who took over as RKO's acting head of production early in 1942. Previously the general manager of RKO Theatres, Koerner was tasked with turning around the fortunes of the ailing studio following a string of box-office failures, the most high-profile of which was *Citizen Kane* (1941). Noting the success that Universal had enjoyed with horror films, Koerner invited Lewton to form a new, low-budget, production unit. Lewton was obliged to work under executive producer Lou Ostrow, use studio-approved titles pre-tested by the Gallup organisation, accept a cap of $150,000 on his budgets and a screen running time of no more than 75 minutes, but he otherwise had a considerable degree of freedom in shaping the subject matter.

It's hard to overstate what a personal gamble this was for Lewton. Married with two young children to support and frequently seized by periods of self-doubt, he nevertheless left his secure job with Selznick for a nominal three-year RKO contract, which actually offered no guarantee of renewal after the first twelve months. Added to that, the USA had entered the war following the attack on Pearl Harbor just three months previously and nobody yet knew what privations might lie ahead. He doubtless saw it as a stepping-stone to a better position in the future but he agonised over the decision, writing to his mother and sister that 'it isn't as good a proposition as it sounds. RKO is a very badly mismanaged and disorganised place and producers, unless their contracts are for a longer period, rarely last more than six months'.[4] He also worried that he'd be unable to achieve anything significant, since he'd be working on 'such wretched and uninteresting material. I'm to do two horror stories and two detective stories, all on very close budgets, with cheap actors, directors and writers. It won't be like working on "Jane Eyre"'.[5] Despite this, Lewton not only grasped the nettle but ultimately chose to do so in a way that entailed even further personal and professional risk. 'They may think I'm going to do the usual chiller stuff which'll make a quick profit, be laughed at and be forgotten', he told Bodeen once he'd settled into his new job, '… but I'm going to do the kind of suspense movie *I* like'.[6]

THE 'HORROR' UNIT

Lewton started work at RKO on Monday, 16 March 1942, and immediately began to build a team around him, 'choos[ing] collaborators who were sympathetic to his personality and vision'.[7] Jessie Ponitz was assigned to be his secretary, to help acquaint him with the lot. Lewton came to rely on her and she, in turn, became extremely protective of the sensitive producer. Lewton's first recruit was writer Bodeen, with whom he'd worked on the development of *Jane Eyre*. A month later he brought in Tourneur. Lewton and Tourneur had developed a close friendship during their work together on *A Tale of Two Cities*, and Tourneur had since established himself as the director of shorts and B features at both MGM and Republic. To advise Lewton on technical matters, Lou Ostrow added editor Mark Robson to the team. The new unit soon became known, affectionately, as 'The Snake Pit'. The final addition to Lewton's original core team was Ardel Wray. At the new producer's request, she was promoted later that summer from her position as the assistant head of the RKO story department, to become his second chosen writer.

From the start, Lewton was an unconventional producer. Unlike many of his contemporaries, he didn't merely supervise a production. Instead, he shaped his stories carefully from conception to release, injecting his personality into each project and essentially 'pre-directing' the film at script stage.[8] Robson described Lewton as 'a benevolent David Selznick'.[9] However, 'where Selznick was perceived as intrusive by those who worked with him, Lewton was regarded by his colleagues as self-effacing, and always willing to give his team creative freedom'.[10] Each member of his tightly knit unit felt they had a personal stake in the finished product. Ponitz said: 'When he asked for your opinion, you felt that he seriously wanted to hear what you had to say … It was the same with everybody else; there was a great sense of collaboration, although it was really, and finally, Val's work.' Wray elaborated:

> I don't think I can explain the particular kind of togetherness (a concept not dear to me) that Val managed then. You can't call it teamwork, because that implies a kind of hearty I'll-be-quiet-while-you-talk-and-then-you'll-be-quiet-while-I-talk situation – all wrong. It wasn't cozy … There were some pretty rugged disagreements. But it was togetherness, all right – really, ideally, in a work sense … more like theatre.[11]

Lewton even brought in, at the earliest possible opportunity, colleagues such as composer Roy Webb – who would normally be consulted only *after* the completion of the picture – inviting his creative input whilst the story was still being shaped.

Nevertheless, assembling a reliable team was only one of the issues Lewton encountered as he sought to build a functioning unit. He soon began to face resistance from the front office to his creative choices, as will be examined in more detail below. Plus, on top of the format constraints he was obliged to work within, wartime restrictions placed additional logistical hurdles in his path. Gasoline rationing impacted RKO more than most other studios owing to the wide geographical spread of its real estate. Raw materials also had to be preserved for the war effort. Initially, a cap of $5,000 was placed on each production for set construction – a restriction later eased to an overall quarterly studio allocation – and even raw film stock was rationed. However, taking the advice of veteran producer Herman Schlom on how best to manage his tight budgets, Lewton cut pre-production costs and made judicious use of existing sets. He fussed over the dressing of the sets that would feature most prominently in each film, creating an impression of high production values that belied the tight budget, and took equal care over the actors' wardrobes, recycling costumes from previous films whenever possible.

Such was Lewton's success at making the most of his limited resources that some have begun to question whether the description of his films as low-budget B movies is accurate, speculating that they may instead have been 'modestly budgeted A features'.[12] However, the new producer and his colleagues were under no illusions that they were working on anything other than B pictures, and the evidence doesn't support the contrary supposition. Precise definitions varied from studio to studio, but RKO used two parameters to define its B product. First was the cost. The B-movie budget ceiling (which applied to the Lewton unit) was imposed because experience had demonstrated that 'B pictures costing more than $150,000 had shown a clear record of losses', and because the more expensive 'medium'-budget or 'in-between' films had proven to be an 'economic liability'.[13] As a result, the budgets of Lewton's first five features were exactly in line with those of RKO's *Mexican Spitfire* B comedy series.[14] The second parameter was the release pattern. *Cat People* was initially leased to exhibitors on the flat-rental basis reserved for B pictures, as opposed to a percentage of box office demanded for A pictures. The status of Lewton's films certainly increased in the wake of his early successes – as did the budgets of his later films – but this was a reward he *earned*, not a deliberate positioning of his films from the start.

Similarly, it's been suggested that Lewton's radical formula – his 'prestige', 'hybrid', 'female-centred' approach to horror – was a strategy pursued by the *studio*, rather than a methodology he devised in the face of opposition.[15] Again, however, there's no evidence to support that view. RKO's primary aim was to produce 'low-cost' pictures that 'should compete successfully with the Universal horror films'.[16] Koerner had first mooted the idea of making 'low-budget horror pictures' as early as December 1941, citing the box-office takings of Universal's *The Wolf Man* (1941) and Fox's *Swamp Water* (1941) in which the 'horror and gruesome angle is stressed very strongly'. What RKO needed, he believed, were commercial 'horror-type' pictures that would do 'exceptionally good business in the so-called B or exploitation houses'.[17] Initially, his suggestion was rebuffed. However, by the time he took over as head of production in 1942, the prevailing mood at RKO was so grim that it 'must have seemed like a besieged medieval township'.[18] It was in this climate that Koerner implemented his plan. The fact that Lewton was contracted to deliver two horror and two *detective* stories during his first year (the latter requirement nominally fulfilled by *The Leopard Man* and *The Seventh Victim*, both 1943) only serves to underline RKO's desperation for purely commercial fodder and is indicative of a studio hedging its bets with the as-yet untested producer. Their desire to ape Universal's output was also demonstrated by the hiring of *Wolf Man* screenwriter Curt Siodmak for *I Walked with a Zombie* and by their attempt to poach Lon Chaney Jr for the lead in *The Leopard Man*.[19] Lastly, if further proof were needed, Lewton's executive producer actively fought *against* the producer's ideas during the making of his first film.

THE LEWTON TOUCH

The foundations of the unique cinematic style that Lewton would further refine for *I Walked with a Zombie* were established during the development and production of *Cat People*.

Koerner assigned Lewton the pre-tested title for his first project during his early days at the studio. Looking to ride on the box-office coattails of *The Wolf Man*, Koerner had conceived the title himself after an informal discussion about horror films in which someone had observed that 'nobody had done much of anything about cats'.[20] Lewton initially considered adapting an existing literary property as the basis for the film, but by the time Bodeen joined him at the studio in April he'd decided to create an original, using aspects of his own short story 'The Bagheeta', published in *Weird Tales* in 1930, about a legendary creature who is half-woman and half-cat. From the beginning Lewton veered away from the Universal formula. He ran for Bodeen 'some American and British horror and suspense movies which were typical of what he did *not* want to do' [emphasis mine]. Rather than a 'Hollywood' kind of horror picture, Lewton wanted a 'more Continental type of story, which opens at a leisurely pace, allowing one to understand and sympathize with the main characters, each sequence growing in suspense'.[21] Ultimately, the two of them devised a refined, oblique, feminised version of *The Wolf Man*, about a Serbian immigrant, Irena, who believes she's cursed to turn into a murderous leopard when her passions are roused. Lewton carried over several basic elements of the *Wolf Man* story – even dropping in a tongue-in-cheek reference to the earlier film – but his treatment of it was a radical departure. It was nothing less than 'an ambitious effort to reform [the] genre's conventions in ways that touch all facets of filmic style'.[22]

> We tossed away the horror formula right from the beginning [said Lewton]. No grisly stuff for us. No masklike faces hardly human, with gnashing teeth and hair standing on end … But take a sweet love story, or a story of sexual antagonisms, about people like the rest of us ... and cut in your horror here and there by suggestion, and you've got something.[23]

His approach was restrained, nuanced and psychological – though the end result was far more than mere 'psychological horror'. Notably, Lewton made a point of positioning women as his lead characters, extremely rare in the horror genre at that time. He'd long demonstrated a preference for female protagonists – for example, in his novels *The Laughing Woman*, *Four Wives* and his most successful prose work *No Bed of Her Own* – a sensibility he shared with David Selznick, who was regarded as 'a "woman's producer," attuned to the … psychology of the American female'.[24] Lewton went on to feature female protagonists in eight of his eleven RKO features.

In addition, acutely aware of home front concerns, he set his stories in 'the reality of the American present, which would become the dominant setting of the horror genre during the war',[25] in contrast to Universal's preference for mythical European settings. His characters were recognisable people with real jobs, and '[w]hile Universal's horror films center around the genre's central signifier, the monster, Lewton's films at RKO diffuse that signifier by rendering ordinary people as potentially monstrous'.[26] While crafting the *Cat People* script, Lewton and Bodeen 'put a touchstone of reality to every scene':

> [W]e always talked of the scene in two ways. One way, the horror way, and the other, as if the horror element were out of it. If it stood up without the horror, we accepted it. If not, we threw it out and tried again. When you read *Cat People*, just substitute either insanity or social disease for Irena's mad beliefs, and you'll see that the story still stands up.[27]

The social dimension introduced into *Cat People* would be expanded in *I Walked with a Zombie*. Lewton was not politically active but was unquestionably liberal by nature, and he and his writers layered a range of resonant, socially conscious themes into all of his subsequent scripts.

Cat People created the blueprint for what would become the Lewton unit's iconic visual style, based around shadows and suggestion. Another technical innovation was the development of the 'bus' – a gradual build-up of screen tension that is abruptly shattered by a loud sound or visual, causing the audience to jump in their seats – named after the sudden arrival of a Central Park bus into the scene in which Irena's love-rival Alice is being stalked by an unseen presence. The device – nowadays known as the 'jump-scare' and, arguably, grossly overused – was utilised sparingly, often during a 'Lewton walk', a perilous extended excursion undertaken by one of the characters.

However, Lewton's war against the conventions of screen horror faced opposition from within. His direct supervisor Lou Ostrow viewed the producer as 'too pretentious and fussy to succeed as a producer of popular entertainment'. He baulked at many of Lewton's early, more avant-garde story concepts, ordered the accounting and security departments to watch for any 'irregularities in protocol' committed by the unit, attempted to have Jacques Tourneur fired after the first few days of shooting on *Cat People* and insisted that Lewton and Tourneur include a visible leopard in a key sequence originally designed to rely on sound and suggestion and show nothing but dark shadows.[28] Despite this, Koerner was ultimately delighted with the pair's efforts in shaping the *Cat People* screenplay, praising it as 'the most intelligent treatment of a popular and fantastic story he had ever read'.[29] Koerner's relationship with Lewton was far more cordial than has sometimes been suggested and, in due course, he began to have doubts about Ostrow's sensibilities – perhaps partly because of the latter's combative relationship with Lewton. Ostrow eventually quit RKO the same month that *I Walked with a Zombie* premiered, after a 'policy dispute' with the front office.[30]

Cat People finally began shooting on 28 July 1942. On the screen, all the elements of Lewton's unique approach to screen horror were combined via 'the visual grace and artistic delicacy which Tourneur used to make screenplays blossom as films'.[31] Simultaneously, veteran cameraman Nicholas Musuraca conjured a 'highly dramatic lighting … now celebrated as the quintessential film noir style',[32] whilst Robson brought to the editing the skills he'd honed on Orson Welles' *Journey into Fear* (1943).

By the end of August, *Cat People* was in the can and undergoing post-production, yet at this stage, no one – least of all Lewton – knew what fate awaited the film once it went into general release. Would a mass audience warm to his delicate and nuanced approach to screen horror? Regardless, *Zombie* was already in development, and Lewton set out to push the narrative and stylistic boundaries even further in his second film. In doing so, he introduced 'what can be called a proto-feminist and proto-decolonial perspective in a popular entertainment genre long before feminist and decolonial studies became part of the academic, intellectual and political discourse'.[33]

Notes

1. See Joel E. Siegel, *Val Lewton: The Reality of Terror* (Secker & Warburg, 1972) and Edmund G. Bansak, *Fearing the Dark: The Val Lewton Career* (McFarland, 2003).
2. DeWitt Bodeen, *More from Hollywood!* (AS Barnes, 1977), 309.

3. Lewton, undated letter *circa* April 1941, The Val Lewton Papers, Manuscript Division, Library of Congress, Washington, DC.
4. Lewton, undated letter *circa* February 1942.
5. Lewton, undated letter established as 5 March 1942.
6. Bodeen, *More from Hollywood!*, 306.
7. Siegel, *Val Lewton*, 23.
8. *Val Lewton: The Man in the Shadows* directed by Kent Jones (Warner Video 2008), DVD.
9. Siegel, *Val Lewton*, 21.
10. Martha P. Nochimson, 'Val Lewton at RKO: The Social Dimensions of Horror', *Cineaste* 31/4 (2006), 12.
11. Siegel, *Val Lewton*, 25, 41.
12. See Kim Newman, *Cat People* (BFI Film Classics, 1999), 1, and Mark Jancovich, 'Hot Profits out of Cold Shivers! Horror, the First Run Market, and the Hollywood Studios, 1938–42' in *Merchants of Menace: The Business of Horror Cinema*, ed. Richard Nowell (Bloomsbury 2014).
13. Richard B. Jewell, *RKO Radio Pictures: A Titan is Born* (University of California Press, 2012), 230.
14. Richard B. Jewell, 'A History of RKO Radio Pictures, Incorporated, 1928–1942' (PhD thesis, University of Southern California, 1978), 761–6.
15. Jancovich, 'Hot Profits out of Cold Shivers!' in Nowell, *Merchants of Menace*.
16. Lewton letter dated 6 August 1942, quoted in Constantine Nasr's commentary, *The Leopard Man* (Shout! Factory 2019) Blu-ray.
17. Jewell, *RKO Radio Pictures*, 235.
18. Jewell, *RKO Radio Pictures*, 246.
19. *Los Angeles Times*, 4 September 1943, A10.
20. George Turner, 'Val Lewton's Cat People', *Cinefantastique* 12/4 (1982), 23.
21. Bodeen, *More from Hollywood!*, 310.
22. Michael Lee, 'Sound and Uncertainty in the Horror Films of the Lewton Unit', in *Music, Sound and Filmmakers*, ed. James Wierzbicki (Taylor & Francis, 2012), 107.
23. Quoted in Siegel, *Val Lewton*, 31.
24. Leonard J. Leff, *Hitchcock and Selznick* (University of California Press, 1987), 37.
25. Tim Snelson, *Phantom Ladies: Hollywood Horror and the Home Front* (Rutgers University Press, 2014), 16.
26. Sarah Reichardt Ellis and Michael Lee, 'Monsters, Meaning, and the Music of Chopin in American Horror Cinema of the 1930s and '40s', *Journal of Musicological Research*, 39/1 (2020), 32.
27. Lewton letter dated 6 August 1942, *The Leopard Man* commentary.
28. Michael H. Price, *Forgotten Horrors, Vol. 10: The Missing Years* (Cremo Studios, 2016), 19.
29. Lewton letter dated 6 August 1942, *The Leopard Man* commentary.
30. *Variety*, 7 April 1943, 5.

31. Joel E. Siegel, 'Tourneur Remembers', *Cinefantastique* 2/4 (1973), 24.
32. Turner, 'Val Lewton's Cat People', 26.
33. Teresa de Lauretis, 'I Walked with a Zombie: Colonialism and Intertextuality', *EUtopias* 21 (2021), 29.

Chapter 2: 'Jane Eyre in the West Indies'

I Walked with a Zombie started life as a one-page, non-fiction, illustrated newspaper article titled 'I Met a Zombie', written by Cleveland-based journalist Inez Wallace and published in the Hearst supplement *The American Weekly* on Sunday, 3 May 1942. At that time, Lewton's B unit had been in existence for only seven weeks and, with *Cat People* already in the works, RKO was on the hunt for story material for his second horror production.

Discussion of Wallace's article in literature relating to the film is often mired in confusion. The title of the piece is frequently misquoted and several authors have mistakenly referred to a text republished in Peter Haining's 1985 anthology paperback *Zombie: Stories of the Walking Dead*, which – although written by Wallace – is *not* the original piece; Haining's citation is incorrect, as is his assumption that Wallace was male.[1] Similarly, Wallace's 'original story by' credit in the film – as opposed to a 'based on an article by' credit – has caused even more bewilderment and speculation. Both issues are clarified below.

Figure 2.1: Betsy meets the Byronic Paul Holland.

13

Wallace's piece was approximately 1,700 words in length and consisted of a first-person 'recollection' in three parts: a discussion about zombies between Wallace and a plantation worker aboard a ship bound for Haiti; an encounter between Wallace and a mindless 'thing' as she was riding through a cane plantation on the island; and a subsequent discussion between Wallace and a 'prominent native physician' who informed her that zombies are indeed real, the victims of a potent drug that 'rots the brain' beyond restoration.[2] Although sensationalist in tone, the piece was presented to the reader as a truthful account of her experiences during a six-month tour of the West Indies.

Wallace, a former actress, had been a writer and entertainment columnist for the *Cleveland Plain Dealer* since the late 1920s and was a frequent visitor to Hollywood. She also wrote regular feature articles for popular magazines such as *Collier's* and *This Week*. Evidently, her 'Zombie' article created quite a stir. It elicited rebuttals from both Rulx Léon, the consul-general of Haiti and a respected Haitian scholar based in New York, and Charles B. Vincent, a *former* consul-general. The day after publication, Léon wrote to the newspaper denouncing Wallace's 'fantastic' tale, stating that the 'Zombi' Wallace had seen was 'assuredly a poor harmless lunatic who should at present be confined to one of the [island's] numerous asylums'. In a second letter, sent directly to Wallace, Léon sought to convince her that she'd been the victim of a hoax. Vincent also wrote directly to Wallace and was even more forthright, accusing her of being full of 'childish imaginations', of '[c]reating discord and ill-feelings among the United Nations' with her 'masterpiece of rigmarole' and of being a 'confirmed enemy of the Allied cause … hypocritical, disgusting, and repulsive'. Wallace replied politely to Léon, regretting that the newspaper story had 'distressed' him but stating that she 'pictured Haiti … exactly as she found it', adding that she wasn't the first person to write about zombies. Referring to Haiti's asylums, she offered to write a follow-up piece about 'the great work done by your government in this matter … [and to] clear up, for all time, the question of Haiti's Zombies'. Léon replied to Wallace, accusing her of deliberately distorting the facts, and there the matter appeared to rest.[3] The strength of feeling behind the correspondence is doubtless a reflection of the fact that, following the attack on Pearl Harbor, Haiti had sided with the USA and declared war on the Axis powers. A former US colony, the island was now independent (although the USA still maintained control over its finances) and under the strategic policy of pan-Americanism pursued by the US government, it commanded respect.

Stories of Haitian zombies had long since seeped into the American consciousness, partly via the occupation of the island from 1915 to 1934, partly through books such as William Seabrook's 1929 travelogue *The Magic Island*, and partly as a result of films such as *White Zombie* (1932) and *The Ghost Breakers* (1940). By 1942, 'Zombie' dresses were available from high school shops, women's hats were made of 'Zombie Straw', 'Zombie' drinks could be ordered from the bar, and a nightclub named 'Zombie Village' had opened in Oakland, California. Nevertheless, Wallace's article – perhaps because of its sensational nature and its nationwide distribution in the Sunday supplements – was perceived as an insult to Haiti and its culture at a particularly sensitive time. Lewton would later navigate similar concerns.

Around the same time, the article attracted the attention of RKO's East Coast story department, headed by veteran story editor Leda Bauer. The piece was circulated internally and an unsigned, undated reader's report described it as '[a]n idea fragment that could be used as the bare nucleus of a horror thriller ... A complete plot would have to be built around this eerie, sinister set up for picture purposes.'[4] Bauer, who'd doubtless been tasked with sourcing material for Lewton's unit, was sufficiently impressed to contact Wallace by telephone with a request to purchase the film rights. Wallace agreed, on the condition that she could also simultaneously submit an original screen story. 'This Zombie material is so highly specialised', Wallace is quoted as saying, 'that unless one knows all the angles it's apt to sound corny'. Bauer agreed, after which Wallace 'worked eight days and nights, keeping awake with black coffee', to write her screen treatment.[5]

WALLACE'S SCREEN STORY

The 29-page story outline, titled *The Zombies Walked with Me*, was duly submitted to RKO's New York story department on 10 June 1942. The following day, an unnamed reader reviewed the document: 'Miss Wallace has turned out an exciting, spine-tingling framework for a horror melodrama ... Of its type, this is excellent picture material.'[6] Bauer subsequently wired Wallace, saying that she liked the story and was recommending that RKO should purchase it. The studio did so on 3 July. Later, however, Lewton stated privately that 'Mr Koerner' had been 'bamboozled into buying' it.[7]

Wallace's outline bears the hallmarks of having been written in haste. The characters are one-dimensional, the plotting loose and it unfolds more like a traditional adventure mystery story – complete with red herrings – than a horror tale. The narrative is built around the three key sequences described in Wallace's original newspaper piece and the protagonist appears to be based on Wallace herself. Perhaps chastened by the complaints she'd received, the setting was changed to a fictional location:

> Phyllis Worthington journeys by ship to 'Midnight Island' in the Caribbean, to join her brother and widowed mother on her father's sugar plantation, having been summoned by a cryptic telegram. Whilst aboard she meets Don Tilden, an engineer, also travelling to the island. Upon arrival, Phyllis learns that her mother had died of a heart attack hours previously. She's also told that the plantation manager, Fred Cooper, recently moved the estate's sugar cane fields to an 'obscure island' to benefit from cheap labour. Cooper, however, refuses to reveal its location. Soon after, Phyllis's brother also dies, again of apparent heart failure, but not before warning Phyllis of 'zombies ... working in the fields.' Suspecting Tilden of being involved and determined to discover what's going on, Phyllis departs on a cruise of the Caribbean, trying to locate the 'obscure island' whilst simultaneously searching for evidence of zombies. Along the way she meets the head of an American medical foundation who reveals to her the 'truth' about zombies – that they are victims of a drug that renders them mindless slaves. Finally locating the island, she finds her father's cane fields being tended by a zombie workforce. Captured by the zombie master, a woman named Celeste, Phyllis is threatened with death. However, Don Tilden – whom she'd wrongly suspected – had followed her trail to the island and rescues her at the last minute.[8]

The story might have made a serviceable 'quickie' for one of the poverty row studios such as Monogram or Republic, but given the approach that Lewton was already applying to *Cat People* it was never likely to meet with his approval. The fact that it had been deemed 'excellent material' by the East Coast story department serves only to underline that RKO's expectations for the output of Lewton's unit were extremely limited. Koerner revised the title from *The Zombies Walked with Me* to the more fluent *I*

I WALKED WITH A ZOMBIE

Walked with a Zombie and presented the story to Lewton. On or about the same time, Lewton was also informed that Universal screenwriter Curt Siodmak had been engaged to write the screenplay.

Mark Robson remembered that 'Lewton's face was white and his manner impossibly gloomy when he returned from that meeting with Koerner', and that he 'spent the rest of the day in a grumpy, irritable mood'.[9] Lewton had been particularly disconcerted by the 'horrible title … wished upon us by Mr Koerner'.[10] However, according to DeWitt Bodeen, 'after a day of gloom, his spirits lifted and he told me with a chuckle: "They may never recognize it, but what I'm going to give them … is *Jane Eyre in the West Indies*."'[11]

Figure 2.2: The 'mad' confined Jessica.

Lewton rated *Jane Eyre* highly. He'd researched the novel in depth for Selznick, appraised the Orson Welles Mercury Theatre radio adaptation and was intimately involved in the development of the film property, which Selznick ultimately sold to 20th Century Fox.[12] The basic set-up of the novel – in which a naïve young woman is hired to work for a Byronic figure whose wife is confined with a mental illness, falling in love with him in the process – would serve as a rough template for *Zombie*. However, in crafting a story of

17

this nature, based in the Caribbean, Lewton was determined to confront the history of slavery inherent to the region. The narrative would therefore be shaped around relevant textual and subtextual themes.

RKO MEETS UNIVERSAL

Despite Lewton's aversion to Universal Pictures' approach to the genre, he initially worked constructively with German-born Curt Siodmak to revise Wallace's story. The brother of director Robert Siodmak, Curt had established his genre credentials at Universal with scripts for *The Invisible Man Returns* and *Black Friday* (both 1940), before being assigned to *The Wolf Man*. Having recently completed the script for the forthcoming *Frankenstein Meets the Wolf Man* (1943), he'd 'become the top fantasist among Hollywood screenwriters'.[13] During the period they worked together, Lewton wrote that Siodmak was 'a very fine and imaginative man'.[14] Similarly, Siodmak described Lewton as 'a lovely guy, very erudite, very interesting', adding that he was 'much more interesting than any of those Universal guys'.[15]

RKO's payroll files indicate that Siodmak began work with Lewton on Monday, 13 July 1942. Lewton's *modus operandi* was to sketch out a rough story and theme, which he then discussed with his writer, agreeing on several key moments that would define the shape of the narrative. On *Cat People*, for example, Lewton and Bodeen initially established a number of 'story points', including two of the three 'necessary horror sequences', after which Bodeen was left to expand the story into a satisfactory whole, 'feeling free to invent new sequences if they came to [him]'.[16] In all likelihood, Lewton and Siodmak approached the *Zombie* story in a similar fashion. There's no record of the exact brief that Lewton discussed with Siodmak, but a *Jane Eyre*-style love element, coupled with the themes discussed above, would have been vital components. However, given that Lewton was simultaneously supervising the final preparations for *Cat People* – obsessing over innumerable last-minute details of the script, casting, costumes, sets and set dressings – it's likely he was unable to devote as much time to *Zombie* as he would have wished.

In interviews given much later, Siodmak made various comments about his work on the film, sometimes contradictory and rarely in much detail. 'Lewton gave me a short story', he said, presumably referring to the Wallace treatment, 'but I never used it'.[17] 'Nobody helped me with *I Walked with a Zombie*. Of course, Lewton and I discussed scenes, and if he objected to something, I came up with an alternative suggestion.'[18] 'After I told Lewton my approach to the film, he promised to leave me alone', he told *Black Mask*. Tellingly, he went on to add that Lewton 'had ideas that *didn't fit my conception* [emphasis mine]'.[19] Elsewhere, however, Siodmak gave the impression of having few clear memories of the work itself, admitting in his autobiography, 'I don't know what the story was about, except that a man was married to a beautiful woman who had become a zombie, a living, walking dead, who couldn't react in bed'.[20] For his part, Lewton recorded no complaints about Siodmak beyond the fact that '[h]e barely writes English … and this puts quite a burden upon me, even more perhaps than I can carry with an untrained young writer like Bodeen'.[21] Nevertheless, once the *Cat People* shoot was under way, Siodmak was left alone to expand the story and write the first draft screenplay.

THE GALLUP REPORT

While Lewton and Siodmak were still shaping the basic narrative, RKO commissioned a survey from George Gallup's Audience Research Institute (ARI). Having invested money in Wallace's story and Siodmak's contract – and given the cultural buzz surrounding the word 'zombie' at that time – it made sense to gather information that might benefit the film's production and promotion. RKO's exclusive contract with ARI for 'continuous audience research' had been signed in March 1940 during the tenure of RKO president George Schaefer – the first such agreement between Gallup and a Hollywood studio. By mid-1942, however, Koerner, a former exhibitor who trusted his own instincts, had begun to question the value of ARI's research and continued using it only because Gallup offered 'three months of free service … in exchange for a one-year extension'.[22] It was during this period that the *Zombie* survey was conducted.

ARI Report 169, dated 24 August 1942, covered three main topics: which of two versions of the *Zombie* story had the greater audience acceptance value; the audience acceptance value of the basic subject matter; and the audience's interpretation of the title. Written by David Ogilvy, ARI's assistant director, the report states in the introduction that ARI had 'discussed *I Walked With A Zombie* with Mr Lewton' after the production had already been scheduled, and the 'main problem therefore was to gather information which might be helpful in making the picture'. (Please note, all quotes in this section, unless otherwise stated, are from ARI Report 169.)[23]

It's possible that Lewton saw value in such research, given that his mentor Selznick had previously utilised Gallup's services on an ad hoc basis. However, his pressing schedule meant that he was obliged to continue working on the story with Siodmak and was unable to wait for the report's conclusions.

The survey questionnaire had presented its respondents with two versions of the screen story:

> In both versions the central characters were a young nurse, a plantation owner, a ship captain, and, of course, the Zombie who was the wife of the planter … in one, the nurse and the planter fell in love, and the ship captain was the threat; in the other, the ship captain and the girl were the love interest, and the plantation owner proved to have administered the poison which had made his own wife a Zombie.

The results of this part of the questionnaire found 'little difference between the two, but a slight advantage for the version in which the ship captain was the malevolent character'. Ogilvy added: 'Actually the difference between the two versions was so slight that the … determining factor influencing audience reaction here is the basic subject matter itself and not the plot details'.

In a separate vote measuring the audience's acceptance of the subject matter, a value of '48 per cent' was established. ARI's story evaluation process broke down survey results into three categories: votes exceeding 60 per cent indicated a 'very valuable piece of property', between 50 and 60 per cent was deemed 'average-to-good', and a story that was rated 'below 50 per cent must be considered a liability to the producer who has the misfortune to invest in it'. Ogilvy pointed out that *Zombie*'s 'value of 48 per cent is so low as to create a serious handicap for an A production'. However, since *Zombie* was intended as a B production, he added: 'We do not yet know whether or not the same standards apply to low budget properties, but it is clear that this property is not likely to be a sleeper'. ARI had proven to be inconsistent at predicting the success or failure of prospective RKO projects and, given the eventual success of the film upon release (*Variety* would later describe it as the '[m]ost smashing sleeper of the season'),[24] it's fortunate that RKO no longer placed as much faith in ARI's results as it once had.

Finally, in its evaluation of prospective ticket-buyers, the report concluded that the story was 'particularly popular with the age-group 12 to 18' and 'somewhat stronger with men than with women'. However, a considerable number of people said they wouldn't see the film 'because they do not like this type'. A separate, 'sizeable group' considered it 'too fantastic'. A third group said it was 'too much' like other films, and that it 'sounded like a second feature'. On the plus side, almost half of the people asked the meaning of the word zombie 'had a sufficiently correct impression to suggest the nature of the picture'.

Regardless, with the delivery of Siodmak's first draft script on the very day the ARI report was completed, the latter was already obsolete.

THE SIODMAK DRAFT

Similar to the Wallace treatment that preceded it, Siodmak's 'first draft continuity' screenplay is a functional B-movie script that might have suited another producer or studio, but it was never likely to satisfy Lewton.

> *Canadian nurse Betty Atkins accepts a position as a companion to a sick woman, Daniella Turell, the wife of a plantation owner on the island of St. Sebastian. En route to the island, Betty meets Frank Randolph, the captain of the small schooner transporting her. When Frank talks about Daniella, Betty realises that Frank is in love with her. On their arrival in St. Sebastian, Betty meets George Turell, her employer, and Daniella, a seemingly mentally-ill woman in a trance-like state. One day, walking on the beach with Daniella, they meet Frank. Frank immediately recognises Daniella's illness; the woman is not insane, she's been given a powerful drug that has destroyed part of her brain and made her a zombie. After a clash between Turell and Frank – during which Frank accuses Turell of having poisoned Daniella – Turell tells Betty how Daniella became a zombie. Afraid that she'd run away, Turell had given her the obscure poison so that she would remain with him forever. But his action had defeated his purpose, for he must now live with a walking corpse. Betty, in an attempt to find a cure for Daniella, takes her to a voodoo priest. However, the priest*

refuses to help, saying Daniella must live with Turell as a perpetual punishment against Turell for his crime. Unable to help her patient, Betty tells Turell that she wants to leave St. Sebastian. Turell pleads with her to stay and Betty, afraid, seemingly agrees. However, she plots with Frank to take her and Daniella away the following night. But to Betty's horror, Turell gives Daniella salt – fatal to zombies – causing her to expire. He then proposes that Betty stay with him as mistress of the island, whilst simultaneously revealing a mad, secret plan; he intends to change all of his servants into zombies so that he can rule them without opposition. The local people attempt to bury Daniella's body with voodoo rites, but a fire breaks out when an angry Turell upsets one of the burial lamps placed around Daniella's body. The flames spread to the sugar cane fields, almost trapping Betty as she attempts to escape. However, she's rescued by Frank whilst Turell perishes in the fire.[25]

Overall, Siodmak's screenplay reads like a variation of Victor Halperin's *White Zombie*. It even contains a scene – in which the zombie Daniella plays the piano 'with mechanical perfection, without feeling or a trace of emotion' – that's practically identical to one in Halperin's film. The script contains several moments that elevate it above potboiler status – including a speech given by the voodoo priest that evokes the poetic words of Maleva in *The Wolf Man* – but it is notably lacking in chills. The only overt moment of horror occurs when Daniella, having been fed salt by Turell, attempts to claw her way back into her grave with her bare hands. There's no ambiguity in Daniella's condition – she truly is a zombie. Betty comes across as a particularly uncaring nurse. At one point, while sunbathing, she treats Daniella as a slave, ordering her to fetch a drink in the knowledge that her patient will blindly obey. She displays little agency, faints helplessly twice and has to be rescued at the end by the limp male 'hero'. Turell, though superficially charming, is actually insane and emerges as nothing more than a caricature. An attempt had been made at establishing an underlying theme relating to oppression, but this is largely confined to Turell's crazed scheme to create a zombie workforce. Especially noteworthy is the complete absence of a romantic entanglement between *any* of the characters, with the *Jane Eyre* dynamic seemingly cast aside. In short, Siodmak's draft differed from the final screen version of the script in every respect – plot, character, theme and tone – and it's hard to avoid the conclusion that Siodmak had veered away from the brief he and Lewton had discussed.

I WALKED WITH A ZOMBIE

Figure 2.3: Carrefour the zombie (Darby Jones).

Lewton thanked Siodmak for his contribution (it appears from Siodmak's autobiography that their relationship remained cordial) but his week-to-week contract was terminated on 24 August 1942, the same day the script had been submitted. Either Lewton read and disliked the script immediately, or he'd already decided that Siodmak was not the person to carry it forward through subsequent drafts. Instead, he turned to a young writer with no previous screen credits.

ENTER ARDEL WRAY

Ardel Wray was born Ardel Mockbee on 28 October 1907, the only daughter of stage and screen actress Virginia Brissac and stage actor Eugene Mockbee. After her mother remarried in 1915, to film director John Griffith Wray, Ardel took her stepfather's surname. Her career in the film industry began around 1930, and she worked in the story departments of various studios for several years. She joined RKO in 1938 and was assigned to the Junior Writing Department. By 1942, she'd worked her way up to a position as the assistant to William Nutt, the acting head of the studio's West Coast story department.[26] Wray probably came to Lewton's attention via her close links to the 'Snake Pit'. She was a long-standing friend of Mark Robson and had previously worked alongside DeWitt Bodeen under Nan Cochrane, the head of the RKO reader's department who was, or would become, one of Wray's closest friends and allies. Nor was Wray a stranger to the horror genre. Whilst employed as a writer at Universal Pictures in 1932, she'd written a draft of the original Robert Florey *Wolf Man* property – intended as a vehicle for Karloff – nine years before it was revived and assigned to none other than Curt Siodmak.[27] Wray was well-read, enthusiastic and could deliver high-quality work quickly. It's evident that Lewton saw in her someone who shared his sensibilities, and who could bring to the script the literate feminine perspective so lacking in Siodmak's draft.

Wray was officially transferred to the Lewton unit on 12 September 1942,[28] though it's likely she'd already been undertaking preparatory work for the film during the three weeks that had elapsed since Siodmak had delivered his script; the start of production had already been pushed back from its original September date and time was short. In addition, since Siodmak's fees had already consumed most of the sum allocated for the script in the budget, Lewton was forced to employ a little fiscal sleight-of-hand, paying Wray from the budget for his third film, *The Leopard Man*. As Wray later recalled, it cost Lewton time and money to start over and rework the script, but he so disliked Siodmak's draft that he did so anyway.[29] With *Cat People* now in post-production, Lewton was finally able to give his full attention to *Zombie*'s screen story.

Wray 'plunged into research on Haitian voodoo, every book on the subject Val could find', she later wrote. 'He was an addictive researcher, drawing out of it the overall feel, mood and quality he wanted, as well as details for actual production.'[30] She consulted Seabrook's *The Magic Island*, among other texts, and Zora Neale Hurston's 1938 ethnographic study *Tell My Horse*. A previously published report that Wray hired Hurston as a consultant on the film has since proved erroneous – the result of a misinterpretation of a poor quality audio recording.[31] However, she did meet both Hurston and actor Paul Robeson around that time. Having read *Tell My Horse*, Wray discussed the book with Lewton and they set up an interview in the hope of getting more detail and perhaps some photographs. Robeson accompanied Hurston to the meeting. Hurston was relatively new to Hollywood but had recently been working at Paramount, while Robeson was actively engaging with studios to improve the representation of black people on screen and combat Hollywood's endemic racism. Wray was able to use much of the material that Hurston provided, though, for obvious reasons, was unable to promise the strict levels of scholarly accuracy in her screenplay that Hurston was asking for. The meeting left a strong impression on Wray, and doubtless influenced her approach to the film.[32]

During the first half of September, Lewton and Wray completely reworked the story. In addition to the narrative components already devised by Lewton, elements of *Rebecca* – a household haunted by the 'dead' wife of the owner, preventing him from moving on with his life with another woman – were brought to the fore. *Rebecca* itself is a veiled reworking of *Jane Eyre*, and Lewton had been highly impressed with du Maurier's novel when he'd first read the galley proofs for Selznick, reporting that 'we have got ourselves a tiger. It is as good as *Jane Eyre* and I think the women will be wild about it.'[33] Once *Zombie*'s basic story was constructed, Wray then wrote an entirely new 'first draft' script – indicative of the fact that Siodmak's nominal first draft had, by now, been entirely side-lined. She worked quickly, delivering her 79-page 'incomplete first draft continuity' script on 29 September, then a complete 'estimating' draft (for budget purposes) the following day. Wray essentially nailed the structure of the finished film with these drafts, and much of the dialogue and action would also be carried through to the final shooting script. Further changes would be made, but Lewton was at last gifted a workable script with fully rounded characters that was in such good shape it could finally be budgeted for production.

Although Siodmak's name was retained in the screen credits for contractual (and perhaps publicity) reasons, it can't be overstated how radically different Wray's script was to the Siodmak draft. The characters came alive on the page as living, breathing people for the first time. Betty was softened to Betsy, a warmer and much more conscientious nurse, and Turell was replaced by Paul Holland, the owner of the plantation but totally unlike his psychopathic predecessor. Daniella was renamed Jessica, in honour of Lewton's secretary Jessie Ponitz. James Rand, Paul's half-brother (changed to Wesley Rand in a subsequent draft), replaced Frank Randolph and brought with him an entirely new family dynamic that was central to the revised story. Mrs Rand, the mother to both, was introduced, as was the character of the calypso singer, who would make a significant cameo appearance. Most important of all, the themes relating to slavery and suffering were properly woven into the narrative for the first time.

Figure 2.4: Saint Sebastian/Ti Misery.

Such is the overall similarity between Wray's estimating draft and the finished film, it's necessary to point out only two major differences. First, the film's 'genuine' zombie character, Carrefour, had not yet been included. Secondly, the script contained a climax that was later dropped entirely. Perhaps inspired by the fate of Thornfield Hall in *Jane Eyre* – and Manderley in *Rebecca* – the Fort Holland plantation is destroyed by fire at the end, as it had been in Siodmak's draft. However, Wray's iteration – markedly different from Siodmak's version – is particularly noteworthy since it features an interesting *reversal* of the situation implied in the completed film, in which Jessica is killed by Rand after a voodoo doll in her image is stabbed by the witch doctor. In Wray's version, the killing of Jessica by Rand instead causes the voodoo doll to topple off a shelf at the Houmfort – the voodoo temple – in turn knocking over a candle that starts the fire, which quickly spreads across the cane fields. Holland is almost trapped by the blaze but is saved by Rand, who dies in the process, having redeemed himself for the affair that had destroyed Paul's marriage to Jessica.[34]

The budget was prepared from Wray's estimating draft. Various interim changes were made to the script during the process, to accommodate, for example, legal notes, and savings that could be achieved by relocating certain scenes or adjusting the proposed sets. Simultaneously, pre-production began in earnest. Myriad preparations were instigated, not least of which was the assembly of the principal cast and crew. Most importantly, Jacques Tourneur was now officially assigned to direct the film, on the strength of his handling of *Cat People*.

TOURNEUR

At that time, Tourneur was engaged by RKO on a film-by-film basis. As a result, his services had been terminated four days after the completion of the *Cat People* shoot. However, there was surely never any doubt that he would direct Lewton's second picture and, by 17 September, he was back on the payroll to prepare for *Zombie*.[35] Of the four directors who worked for Lewton at RKO, Tourneur was unquestionably the best, bringing to the productions a coherence and visual flair that the others were never quite able to match.

'Tourneur was an artist of atmospheres', Martin Scorsese wrote, '... with a profound sensitivity to light and shadow, and a very unusual relationship between characters and environment'.[36] His 'directorial touch is exact but disconcertingly light. He makes everybody else look overemphatic.'[37] Although a master of composition he claimed he 'never look[ed] in the camera – cameramen hate a director who is always looking in that thing – because I know pretty well what's in it. But I'm very adamant and descriptive about the source of lighting.'[38] Tourneur disliked unusual camera angles and distorting lenses and focused primarily on achieving a 'strong visual unity by using a type of framing and camera movement that is very simple'. He urged actors to keep their voice low and underplay their performances, 'controlling the tone of the voice and the speed of the delivery'. He added, 'I have always tried to control the sound, but especially the silences in my films'.[39] On this latter point, according to author Paul Willemen, Tourneur's 'orchestration of silences' also extends to images, 'where, according to classic rules of substitution (metaphor), silences are represented as areas of darkness'. Willemen defines this as a 'shadow barrier between the space of the viewer and the diegesis',[40] introducing a threatening 'blind spot' into the image – the incarnation on screen of the Lewton unit's goal of suggestive, unseen horror. 'If you make the screen dark enough', said Lewton, 'the mind's eye will read anything into it you want. We're great ones for dark patches.'[41]

Inevitably, in any discussion of Tourneur's collaboration with Lewton, the question of authorship arises. Most critics and film historians conclude that Lewton was the author of his RKO films – a rare example of the *producer auteur*. Author Chris Fujiwara, however, is a notable exception. Fujiwara contends that Tourneur's directorial style and thematic concerns were already established prior to *Cat People*. Nevertheless, *Cat People* unquestionably elevated Tourneur to an entirely new level, and his post-Lewton career, which *arguably* demonstrated a coherent personal approach across several genres, does not automatically qualify him as the author of the three films he directed for Lewton, nor of the overall Lewton *oeuvre*. Joel Siegel noted that 'Tourneur is a superb film stylist and interpreter' but doubted 'a very strong case can be made for Tourneur as the prime mover of the Lewton–Tourneur pictures'. He added that 'Robin Wood's tortured attempt to do so in … *Film Comment* reinforces this conclusion'.[42] In fact, even Wood's 'tortured' piece concluded that Tourneur's visual style is 'simply *applied* to the subject matter externally, without in any way transforming it'.[43] Similarly, Claire Johnson and Paul Willemen state that 'traditional *auteurism* has been unable to come to terms with Tourneur's films', and that it's 'impossible to consider Tourneur as an artist expressing a coherent world-view, a coherent and individual thematic'.[44] *Auteur* theorist Andrew Sarris concurred, ranking Tourneur in the third category of his pantheon of directors in *The American Cinema*.

Tourneur himself rather muddied the water for those wishing to analyse his work, via a number of questionable claims made in later years. For example, in an interview with Bertrand Tavernier in 1971, he stated that he'd personally 'initiated' *Zombie*:

> One day I said to Val Lewton, 'I have an idea. We are going to take *Jane Eyre* and we're going to do a remake of it without telling anyone, simply by radically changing the setting.' And that is how *I Walked with a Zombie* came about.[45]

I WALKED WITH A ZOMBIE

Some authors accepted this statement at face value, but it is patently false. Indeed, Tourneur had already said several years earlier that 'I've never in my whole life initiated a film – I've always taken what they've given me'.[46] Similar claims he made about *Cat People*, perhaps resulting from a genuinely faulty memory, also fall apart under close examination. Nevertheless, nothing can be taken away from the profound contribution Tourneur made to his three Lewton films, nor from the influence that he exerted on the directors who followed in his wake.

Concerning *Zombie* specifically, it's impossible to isolate Tourneur's creative input to the *development* of the project, given that the entire unit constantly bounced around ideas during the scripting process. Although he was off the payroll during the crucial period in which Wray and Lewton broke the final screen version of the story, it's possible he was consulted on an informal basis. His contributions to the actual production, however, are analysed in Chapter Three.

KEY ROLES

English actress Anna Lee had been Lewton's first choice to play Betsy, as far back as July when the project had been announced. However, following a delay to the start of production, and a subsequent clash of shooting schedules, Lewton was forced to look for a last-minute replacement. (Lee later starred alongside Karloff in Lewton's *Bedlam*.) Frances Dee, married to actor Joel McCrea, was cast instead. Tom Conway, who'd made a lasting impression in *Cat People*, took the lead male role as Paul Holland. James Ellison owed RKO a picture on his contract at the time and consequently played Wesley Rand, while Edith Barrett, who was three years younger than Conway and only three years older than Ellison, was nevertheless cast as their mother. James Bell took the role of Dr Maxwell and, finally, Czech actress Christine Gordon was given her Hollywood debut as Jessica. Information about these lead players is readily available, so the focus here is on the black actors and performers, some of whom are rarely, if ever, discussed.

For the pivotal role of the calypso singer, and to compose special music for the film, Lewton engaged the popular Trinidadian entertainer and poet Sir Lancelot – the stage name of Lancelot Victor Pinard, a musician who'd made a name for himself performing calypso at the Village Vanguard club in New York, the popularity of which eventually led to a West Coast tour. This, in turn, led to a film appearance in Columbia's *Two Yanks in Trinidad* (1942). Lewton first approached Sir Lancelot in September to write the song 'Shame and Sorrow' that he'd later perform in the film, and the lyrics were duly delivered in time to be inserted into the 12 October final draft of the script. (The song has since been covered by countless artists, becoming something of a cultural touchstone.)

Figure 2.5: *Calypso singer (Sir Lancelot)*.

Although he appeared in only one sequence, Sir Lancelot's contribution to the film cannot be overstated. More than any other character in the picture, he gives voice to the simmering resentment felt by the island's community towards the Holland family and its history (see Chapter Three), leaving an indelible impression. Little wonder, then, that Lewton went on to engage Sir Lancelot for *The Ghost Ship* (1943) and *Curse of the Cat People* (1944). His role in the latter film was described by critic James Agee as 'one of the most unpretentiously sympathetic, intelligent, anti-traditional, and individualized Negro characters I have ever seen presented on the screen'.[47]

Having secured the services of Sir Lancelot, Lewton wrote the following memo to Lou Ostrow a week before production started: 'I am very anxious to engage Mr Antoine, the Haitian drummer and musician, as a technical director ... to guide us in choosing authentic music and help stage the dances and ceremonial business in the Houmfort scenes'.[48] LeRoy Antoine, who'd co-authored with Laura Bowman the 1938 book *The Voice of Haiti*, was subsequently engaged. He supplied genuine voodoo songs for the film and choreographed the set-piece Houmfort musical sequence, ensuring it was both authentic and respectful. Antoine briefly appeared in the film and also helped to promote the picture. His contribution was highlighted in the film's press book – along with his knowledge and views on both voodoo and zombies – the contents of which ran in several newspapers. In addition, Antoine facilitated the engagement of several actors and dancers for the Houmfort sequence.

Jeni LeGon featured prominently in these scenes. Born in Georgia, she had been the first African American woman to sign with a major studio – MGM – though her film debut had been in RKO's *Hooray for Love* (1935). Despite her groundbreaking contract, MGM dropped her from *Broadway Melody of 1936* (1935) in favour of Eleanor Powell, on the basis that they 'couldn't have two tap dancers in the [same] picture'. LeGon suspected the real reason was her race. She was warmly received in England subsequently, appearing at the Adelphi and in the British film *Dishonour Bright* (1936). Back in the USA, she appeared in numerous films over the next 17 years, usually in demeaning minor roles, and she finally quit Hollywood in 1953, soon after an unsuccessful campaign against the stereotyping of black actors in film.[49]

Taking the part of the Sabreur – witch doctor – was Panama-born Jieno Moxzer. He'd appeared on Broadway in *Cabin in the Sky* in 1940, and reprised his role in the MGM film version in 1942. He also appeared in the play *Dakar Speaks*, at LA's Beaux Arts Theatre in 1942. He was involved in government-funded arts projects and taught community dance for most of his life, from the 1930s to the 1970s.[50] He brought a sinuous, menacing presence to his role.

Joining LeGon in the second of two Houmfort dance sequences was Kathleen Hartsfield, about whom, sadly, very little is known. Hartsfield – apparently also a model – appeared in *Cabin in the Sky* alongside Moxzer, and also in *Stormy Weather* (1943) and *Broadway Rhythm* (1944). Trinidad-born Rita Christiani, a dancer with the Katherine Dunham Company who performed in several films, had originally been lined up for this sequence but was replaced by Hartsfield for unspecified reasons. However, she briefly appeared elsewhere in the film. Vivian Dandridge, a singer, dancer and actress, and the daughter of Ruby Dandridge, appeared in a cameo, playing the character of Melise.

Filling the small but important role of Alma was veteran actress Theresa Harris (credited as Teresa on screen). Fresh from her part in *Cat People*, she had appeared in scores of films following her first role in *Thunderbolt* (1929) – most notably in the pre-Code picture *Baby Face* (1932), in which she shared equal screen time with star Barbara Stanwyck. She was a talented singer and dancer, consistently memorable in her performances despite being frequently typecast as a maid. She continued acting in both film and television until 1958. Harris brought a dignified and knowledgeable presence to her part.

Lastly, Darby Jones was cast in the iconic role of Carrefour (also spelt Carre-Four). Los Angeles-born Jones was a former athlete who appeared in numerous films, usually in uncredited bit parts, starting with *Tarzan the Fearless* in 1933. Notable appearances included *Tarzan Escapes* (1936) and the Marx Brothers' *A Day at the Races* (1937) Again, little is known about his life beyond the screen, but it appears he was later involved in union activism for the Worker's Alliance, along with his wife, and he drew the attention of the House Un-American Activities Committee in 1945.[51] Alexander Nemerov devotes an entire chapter to the Carrefour character in his book *Icons of Grief: Val Lewton's Home Front Pictures*.

Of the crew, Lewton carried over from *Cat People* all of his key technicians, with the exception of J. Roy Hunt, who was appointed Director of Photography in place of the unavailable Nicholas Musuraca. Simultaneously, while juggling the complex logistics involved in setting up the production, Lewton also had to navigate the censorship requirements of the PCA, and the political sensitivities of the Office of War Information (OWI).

THE PCA, THE OWI AND THE BMP

Joseph Breen's PCA enforced the Motion Picture Production Code, a strict set of moral guidelines that defined acceptable content for all motion pictures released in the United States. (The PCA was also known informally as the Breen Office and the Hays Office. The two former terms are used interchangeably in this volume.) As noted in Chapter One, Lewton had established an extremely cordial working relationship with Breen while working for Selznick, to the extent that Lewton considered him a personal friend. However, now that he was at RKO, Lewton was obliged to filter all his correspondence with Breen through William Gordon, RKO's production code executive. RKO submitted the 'final' script for *Zombie* to the PCA on 13 October 1942. Lewton and Wray had already made several revisions to the script, the most significant of which was the removal of the fiery climax, which had likely been deemed impossible to achieve satisfactorily on the limited budget. Also, since Jessica Holland's status as a 'zombie' was always intended to be ambiguous, an apparently 'genuine' zombie character, Carrefour, had now been woven into the story.

The Breen Office replied to RKO two days later. Whilst reporting that 'the basic story seems to meet the requirements of the production code', they pointed out several specific objections, largely relating to drinking and 'gruesomeness'. The most significant note, which would be raised repeatedly during script revisions, urged that the climax should 'not suggest that Rand has committed suicide … Since he is a murderer, this is an essential change.' One of the primary stipulations of the Code was that murderers must be seen to be punished by the law, and any hint of suicide in this instance would be perceived as the 'villain' evading the law. Of more immediate import, however, was the following suggestion: 'We urge and recommend that you consult Mr Watterson Rothaker as to the attitude of his board with reference to the export license for this type of entertainment at this time'. This was a reminder that Rothaker's Los Angeles Board of Review, the local branch of the Office of Censorship, had the ability to refuse overseas distribution of the film. The point was reinforced in the next paragraph: 'We think also that some consideration should be given to the possibility of having the locale of this story in Africa rather than in the West Indies … this for possible reactions of the countries in the West Indies region'. A further blunt note of warning, this time regarding the domestic market, was added: 'We presume you have given some thought to the possible reactions of the negroes in this country to a story of this sort dealing with voodoo practices by coloured people'.[52] Lewton and Wray had indeed given a great deal of thought to such issues, but the PCA advice was nevertheless being extended to any film at that time dealing with the representation of black people on screen, against a backdrop of extreme sensitivity from the OWI.

In the aftermath of Pearl Harbor, the US government began liaising with Hollywood to ensure the studios honoured their pledge to help the war effort. The Bureau of Motion Pictures (BMP) was subsequently established in April 1942, run by Lowell Mellett and his deputy Nelson Poynter, to act as 'the clearing house for all dealings between the studios and government'.[53] The BMP had no censorship powers. Instead, it aimed to *shape* the content of Hollywood motion pictures. When the BMP was taken under the umbrella of the newly formed OWI in June 1942, director Elmer Davis stated: 'The easiest way to inject a propaganda idea into most people's minds is to let it go in through the medium of an entertainment picture when they do not realize they are being propagandized'.[54] To this end, in the summer of 1942 the BMP/OWI (henceforth OWI) issued the 'Government Information Manual for the Motion Picture Industry', which consisted of 'a comprehensive statement of OWI's vision of America, the war, and the world'.[55] Each studio was expected to embrace the ideals outlined in the document and reflect them in their films. Hollywood remained wary, but most of the studios – with the notable exception of Paramount – went along with a voluntary scheme that enabled the OWI to review scripts ahead of production and comment upon the content. Increasingly, however, the OWI began to apply pressure on studios to change motion pictures that contained, in their view, objectionable content. The resultant tussle between the two sides continued in the background during the making of *Cat People* and *Zombie*.

One of the OWI's aims was to project the image of the United States as a unified, democratic society facing a common fascist enemy. It encouraged films 'that showed women and blacks as full participants in the war effort who were benefitting from the resultant gains', and was particularly 'sensitive about the depiction of home-front race relations' and the 'evocation of America and its democratic allies' histories of slavery and imperialism'.[56] By the time the first draft of *Zombie* was being written in August 1942, the OWI's approach to the issue of slavery had already been set in stone. That same month, OWI's chief film analyst Dorothy Lloyd wrote in her script review of the proposed MGM film *Battle Hymn*: 'The fact that slavery existed in this country is certainly something which belongs in the past and which we wish to forget at this time when unity of all races and creeds is all-important'.[57] However, the end result of the OWI's attempts to micromanage the situation was that black characters were often written out of films entirely. For example, in the case of *Battle Hymn*, rather than depict a group of blacks in a Civil War household who 'would probably be perceived as slaves', the OWI recommended that they be deleted from the script wholesale.[58] Instead of grappling with a complex depiction of a black character in *Action in the North Atlantic*, Warner Brothers 'simply eliminated him, sidestepping the issue'.[59]

It appears that RKO managed to avoid showing the *Zombie* script to the OWI before it went into production, but Lewton had nevertheless been cautious. To avoid any potential offence to Haiti and its people, he'd removed from the 29 September script a reference to a real-life zombie-related clause in the island's penal code, which outlawed the use of 'poisoning' to produce a 'prolonged state of lethargy'.[60] Later, during production, he admonished a journalist who'd asked, during a visit to the set, if the setting of the film was meant to be Haiti: 'For heaven's sake don't say that … We've been very careful in the story not to identify the island.'[61] Nevertheless, he was determined not to water down the condemnation of slavery that had been woven into the story, and the inevitable encounter with the OWI is discussed in Chapter Four below.

PRODUCTION

On Monday, 24 October 1942, less than six months after the publication of Wallace's newspaper article, the cameras finally rolled on *I Walked with a Zombie*. Tourneur's unit moved between the Houmfort and cane field sets, which had been built on soundstages at the RKO Pathé lot in Culver City (now Amazon Studios), and the Fort Holland sets on RKO's Gower Street lot (now Paramount). In addition, exterior standing sets on the (long-since demolished) 40 Acres backlot in Culver City were repurposed as St Sebastian, and coastal scenes were shot on location in Malibu.[62]

As per his usual practice, Lewton had polished the final draft of the script prior to production – emboldened in his efforts, most likely, by a positive audience preview of

Cat People earlier that month – and he continued making last-minute page revisions, obsessing over details, throughout the shoot. During this time, he continued to fight the PCA over the 'suicide' of Wesley Rand at the end of the film, eventually overcoming their objection by introducing Carrefour into the scene, to give the appearance that the zombie pursues Rand into the ocean. Nevertheless, the scene, as shot, remains ambiguous. Tourneur's unit finally wrapped on 19 November, four days behind schedule.

Since Tourneur's picture deal did not include final cut, his services were signed off on 23 November, four days after the completion of the shoot. Nevertheless, Lewton, who supervised Mark Robson's edit of the film, would almost certainly have continued to consult Tourneur during the process. Several significant changes were made in post-production that would reshape the narrative and the overall tone of the film still further. These revisions are covered in the analysis of the film's final text in Chapter Three.

Notes

1. Peter Haining, ed., *Zombie: Stories of the Walking Dead* (Target Books, 1985), 17.
2. Inez Wallace, 'I Met a Zombie', *American Weekly*, 3 May 1942, 90.
3. Container 1, Folder 3, MS 4477, Inez Wallace and Frank Hubbell Papers, Western Reserve Historical Society, Cleveland, Ohio.
4. Undated reader's report, *I Met a Zombie*, RKO Radio Pictures Records (Collection PASC 3). UCLA Library Special Collections, Charles E. Young Research Library, University of California, Los Angeles.
5. Inez Wallace, 'Inez Gives the Inside Story', *Cleveland Plain Dealer*, 4 April 1943, 17-B.
6. Reader's report dated 11 June 1942, *The Zombies Walked with Me*, RKO Records.
7. Lewton letter dated 6 August 1942, quoted in Constantine Nasr's commentary, *The Leopard Man* (Shout! Factory 2019) Blu-ray.
8. Screen story dated 10 June 1942, *The Zombies Walked with Me*, RKO Records.
9. Joel E. Siegel, *Val Lewton: The Reality of Terror* (Secker & Warburg, 1972), 41.
10. Lewton letter dated 6 August 1942, *The Leopard Man* commentary.
11. DeWitt Bodeen, *More from Hollywood!* (AS Barnes, 1977), 314.
12. Thomas Schatz, *The Genius of the System: Hollywood Filmmaking in the Studio Era* (Pantheon Books, 1998), 328.
13. Gregory William Mank, *It's Alive! The Classic Cinema Saga of Frankenstein* (Tantivy Press, 1981), 112.
14. Lewton letter dated 6 August 1942, *The Leopard Man* commentary.

15. Tom Weaver, *Return of the B Science Fiction and Horror Heroes: The Mutant Melding of Two Volumes of Classic Interviews* (McFarland, 2000), 306.
16. Bodeen, *More from Hollywood!*, 310.
17. Lee Server, *Screenwriter: Words Become Pictures* (Main Street Press, 1987), 223.
18. Weaver, *Return of the B Science Fiction and Horror Heroes*, 306.
19. 'Curt Siodmak: The Black Mask Interview', accessed 16 December 2021, https://blackmaskmagazine.com/blog/curt-siodmak-the-black-mask-interview/.
20. Curt Siodmak, *Wolf Man's Maker: Memoir of a Hollywood Writer* (Scarecrow Press, 2001), 282.
21. Lewton letter dated 6 August 1942, *The Leopard Man* commentary.
22. Susan Ohmer, *George Gallup in Hollywood* (Columbia University Press, 2006), 159.
23. Audience Research Institute Report 169, *Gallup Looks at the Movies: Audience Research Reports 1940–1950* (American Institute of Public Opinion & Scholarly Resources, Inc., 1979).
24. *Variety*, 14 April 1943.
25. *I Walked with a Zombie*, first draft continuity, 24 August 1942, RKO Records.
26. Clive Dawson, 'Ardel Wray: Val Lewton's Forgotten Screenwriter', *Bright Lights*, 26 December 2018, accessed 22 March 2023, https://brightlightsfilm.com/ardel-wray-val-lewtons-forgotten-screenwriter/.
27. Gregory William Mank, Philip Riley and George Turner, *The Wolf Man* (MagicImage Filmbooks, 1993), 24.
28. Payroll cards, RKO Records.
29. Wray family history, courtesy of Stefani Warren, executor of the estate of Ardel Wray.
30. Siegel, *Val Lewton*, 41.
31. Catherine A. Stewart, *Long Past Slavery: Representing Race in the Federal Writers' Project* (University of North Carolina Press, 2016), 242.
32. Wray family history.
33. Schatz, *The Genius of the System*, 276.
34. *I Walked with a Zombie*, first draft continuity – incomplete, 29 September 1942, and estimating script, 30 September 1942, RKO Records.
35. Payroll cards, RKO records.
36. Chris Fujiwara, *Jacques Tourneur: The Cinema of Nightfall* (McFarland, 2011), XI.
37. Geoffrey O'Brien, 'Artisan of the Unseen', *Film Comment* 38/4 (2002), 48.
38. Jacques Tourneur, 'Taste Without Clichés', *Films and Filming* 12/2 (1965): 9–11, 9.
39. Clare Johnston and Paul Willemen, *Jacques Tourneur* (Edinburgh Film Festival, 1975), 48–57.
40. Johnston and Willemen, *Jacques Tourneur*, 16–35.
41. *Los Angeles Times*, 28 March 1943.
42. Joel E. Siegel, 'Tourneur Remembers', *Cinefantastique* 2/4 (1973): 24–25, 24.
43. Robin Wood, 'The Shadow Worlds of Jacques Tourneur', *Film Comment* 8/2 (1972): 64–70, 64.
44. Johnston and Willemen, *Jacques Tourneur*, 5.

45. Johnston and Willemen, *Jacques Tourneur*, 56.
46. Tourneur, 'Taste Without Clichés', 11.
47. James Agee, *Agee on Film* (Modern Library, 2000), 70.
48. Memo from Val Lewton to Lou Ostrow dated 20 October 1942, RKO Records.
49. *Independent*, 21 January 2013.
50. 'City Scene', City of Sacramento Public Information Office (Radio), 3 April 1979.
51. *1945 Report by the California Joint Fact-Finding Committee on Un-American Activities*, 145.
52. Correspondence, *I Walked with a Zombie*, Production Code Administration Records, Margaret Herrick Library, Los Angeles, California.
53. Clayton R. Koppes and Gregory D. Black, *Hollywood Goes to War: How Politics, Profits and Propaganda Shaped World War II Movies* (University of California Press, 1990), 67.
54. Koppes and Black, *Hollywood Goes to War*, 74.
55. Koppes and Black, *Hollywood Goes to War*, 76.
56. Tim Snelson, *Phantom Ladies: Hollywood Horror and the Home Front* (Rutgers University Press, 2014), 41.
57. Koppes and Black, *Hollywood Goes to War*, 142.
58. Koppes and Black, *Hollywood Goes to War*, 179.
59. Koppes and Black, *Hollywood Goes to War*, 115.
60. Barbara Bavis, 'Does the Haitian Criminal Code Outlaw Making Zombies', In Custodia Legis, Library of Congress Blogs, 31 October 2014, accessed on 17 December 2021, https://blogs.loc.gov/law/2014/10/does-the-haitian-criminal-code-outlaw-making-zombies/.
61. *Charlotte Observer*, 1 December 1942, 18.
62. Production files, *I Walked with a Zombie*, RKO Records.

CHAPTER 3: I WALKED WITH A ZOMBIE

The film opens with the RKO radio tower logo, accompanied by Roy Webb's wartime fanfare – a variation of the opening of Beethoven's Fifth Symphony representing the three dots and single dash of the Morse code letter 'V' for 'Victory' – which then segues into Webb's main title music. The elegant, superimposed title cards are presented in Caslon Old Style, Lewton's preferred font, which he used for six of his nine RKO thrillers, eschewing the 'goddamn "fur" letters and other trick lettering that gave one a supposed sense of horror'.[1]

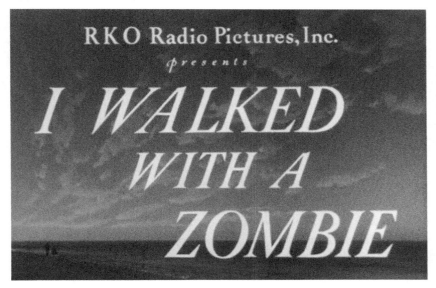

Figure 3.1: Front titles.

Under the titles, we see a perspective shot of a beach beneath wispy matte-painted clouds. Along the shoreline, two distant silhouetted figures approach, a tall thin man and a woman in a nurse's cloak. It will eventually become apparent that these are the film's protagonist, Betsy Connell (Frances Dee) and the 'zombie' Carrefour (Darby Jones). The scene is idyllic and evocative, the characters walking together serenely – the exact opposite of what one might expect for the opening of a 'horror' film. Similarly, Webb's score is romantic rather than ominous. In Wray's early drafts the two figures were Betsy and Jessica, approaching along 'a road spectrally long and straight like a vista in a Dali painting',[2] but this was changed by Lewton to make full use of Tourneur's Malibu location shoot. If it's assumed this walk actually took place – as opposed to the shot being purely symbolic – it raises a question: where does this moment fit into the narrative? As we'll glean from the events that subsequently unfold, it has no place in the story and can only have occurred, if at all, *after* the conclusion of the film. In that respect it punctuates Betsy's *Rebecca*-type voice-over, which begins after the main theme, recounting a story that has already played out. 'I walked with a zombie,' she states, followed by a nervous laugh. 'It does seem an odd thing to say.' The preview audience at the Hawaii Theatre in Hollywood responded to Betsy's words with 'titters', according to the *Motion Picture Herald*,[3] though this was likely what Lewton had intended – inviting viewers to scoff at the trashy title that had been imposed on him before slowly drawing them into the story. Supporting this assumption is the standard disclaimer used in the titles, which was adapted to state: 'Any similarity to actual persons, living, dead *or possessed*, is purely coincidental' (italics in original). Betsy's narration guides us into the story with the words 'it all began in such an ordinary way …'

The next sequence is the only one in the final cut of the film that takes place away from the West Indies. As the snow falls, we're shown the exterior of the 'Parrish & Burden Sugar Company Ltd.', in Ottawa, Canada. The name wasn't chosen at random. It evokes both a 'parish', a small administrative district of both church and state, and the dictionary definition of burden as 'something that is exacting, oppressive',[4] a combination that will come to be associated with the island of St Sebastian, Betsy's ultimate destination. Betsy's nationality was also a deliberate choice, Canada contrasting markedly with the Caribbean in both climate and culture – a binary opposition – emphasising Betsy's status as an outsider.

Within, Betsy is being interviewed for a job, though we initially focus on her interviewer, Mr Richard Brindsley Wilkens, VC, (Alan Edmiston).[5] It's unusual to see characters with disabilities in films of this period, but Wilkens has only one arm, his left coat-sleeve empty. On the wall to the right of Wilkens' desk is what seems to be a portrait of Nelson, who was similarly disabled. Although Wilkens appears in only this one short scene, Wray's script describes him in precise detail, a testament to the attention

I WALKED WITH A ZOMBIE

that was given even to minor characters. The scripted fact that he's a Victoria Cross recipient is not shared with the audience, but the portrait of Nelson, plus the Canadian setting, both hint that St Sebastian may be a member of the British Commonwealth. (However, as discussed below, Lewton had originally wanted the island to be under US administration.) The scene runs for less than one minute yet it packs in a tremendous amount of exposition. Wilkens asks Betsy the usual questions about her marital status and training before hesitating, embarrassed, over one final, 'irregular' question: 'Do you believe in witchcraft?' Betsy laughs dismissively and only then is she told that the job on offer is based on an island in the West Indies. Betsy baulks, until Wilkens points out the advantages – 'Sit under a palm tree … go swimming … take sunbaths' – after which, she's hooked. With the snow falling outside the window, she wistfully repeats to herself, 'palm trees', betraying both her romantic streak and a hint of the naïvety that she'll later display.

Figure 3.2: Interview.

Betsy's Journey

The tone shifts markedly in the next scene, which is bathed in sadness. Over a nighttime shot of a schooner at sea, we hear a slow, mournful song.

> O Marie Congo
> Glo la couleé nan zieu moin
> Quan moin songeé man man moin
> Glo la couleé nan zieu moin.[6]

This authentic Haitian song – a prayer to the Virgin Mary – translates as 'O Congo Mary/My eyes are filled with tears/When I think of my mother/My eyes fill with tears'. As we cut to a view aboard the boat we realise that the song was possibly intended to be diegetic, sung by black deckhands sitting around a stove, heating coffee and grilling meat. Above them stands the boat's captain, at the wheel. Also, with his back to us, is the male protagonist of the film, Paul Holland (Tom Conway). Tourneur's staging of Holland is significant: whilst the captain looks ahead, Holland stares backwards from the rear of the boat, exemplifying the character we'll come to understand as a man who's constantly looking backwards, shackled to the past by family history and unable to move forward with his life owing to circumstances that may or may not be the result of his actions. The deckhands in the lower half of the frame stare at the stove, lost in melancholy thought, and the image symbolically foreshadows the words uttered later by the coachman driving Betsy to Fort Holland, who speaks of his ancestors, brought to the island 'chained to the bottom of the boat'. Next, we're shown Betsy, staring out to sea. Her narration begins to describe the beauty of her surroundings – but Holland abruptly interrupts her thoughts. 'It's not beautiful' (see Figure 2.1). A character in a film replying directly to the voice-over of another is a jarring and unusual moment, perhaps inspired by a similar (though not identical) moment in Welles' *The Magnificent Ambersons*. Holland counters Betsy's perception with his own:

> It's easy enough to read the thoughts of a newcomer. Everything seems beautiful because you don't understand. Those flying fish – they're not leaping for joy. They're jumping in terror. Bigger fish want to eat them. That luminous water. It takes its gleam from millions of tiny dead bodies. The glitter of putrescence. There's no beauty here – only death and decay.

The speech is pure Lewton and sets up one of the key themes of the film – that nothing is as it seems. Betsy's voice-over continues. She reflects on the 'cruelty and hardness' in Holland's voice, concluding that there's something about him that's 'clean and honest – but hurt. Badly hurt.'

A lap-dissolve takes us to the bustling port village of St Sebastian in the morning light. Betsy walks down the schooner's gangplank and across the busy plaza, eventually boarding a horse and trap for the final leg of her journey. The final shooting script contains the following stage direction: 'Over the doorway of one of the buildings – evidently an administrative office – hangs an American flag, indicating the government of the island'. It's not known whether the flag was shown in the background of the raw footage and subsequently deleted, or was dropped before the set was dressed. Its inclusion in the script indicates that Lewton wished to directly associate the island's dark history of slavery with the United States, but the OWI's extreme sensitivity to the issue doubtless made its removal advisable. In its absence, the earlier hint of links to Britain, augmented later in the film by Sir Lancelot's rendition of 'The British Grenadiers', effectively positions the island as a relic of Empire. However, the Dutch and French slave trades are also subtly alluded to via, respectively, the name of the plantation, 'Fort Holland', and the French-derived lyrics of LeRoy Antoine's Haitian songs.

An elderly black coachman (Clinton Rosemond) chats to Betsy *en route* to Fort Holland. He explains that the 'most old' Holland family 'brought the coloured people to the island' as slaves to work the sugar cane. This is the first of two specific verbal references to slavery in the film. The figurehead of the ship that brought them – a statue of Saint Sebastian nicknamed Ti-Misery by the locals – now stands in the garden at Fort Holland, 'an old man ... with arrows stuck in him and a sorrowful weeping look on his black face' (see Figure 2.4). Betsy – naïvely rather than obtusely – replies that 'they brought you to a beautiful place'. Film historian Gwenda Young describes the coachman's reply, 'If you say, Miss, if you say', as 'polite, yet also contemptuous of her ignorance' – a subtle form of 'answering back'. Young cites *Zombie* as being 'a radical film for its time' because of its 'exploration of the idea of *resistance*':

> This resistance is expressed in many forms: from the blacks' refusal to give up the practice of their religion, to the singing of the song by the calypso singer Sir Lancelot.

Tourneur and Lewton refuse to reduce any of the black actors to 'eye-rolling' mumbling caricatures. The blacks may be socially inferior (most of them are maids/ servants) but in no way are they portrayed as morally or intellectually inferior. Black actors are given important roles in the film, very often undercutting white discourse.[7]

Betsy has yet to absorb the underlying truth that Holland had tried earlier to instil in her whilst on the boat, but she'll gradually lose some of her naïvety and 'cultural myopia'.[8]

FORT HOLLAND

As Betsy and the coachman arrive at Fort Holland we're treated to an establishing shot of the gated compound where most of the events of the film will play out. This is part studio set, designed by art directors Albert S. D'Agostino and Walter E. Keller, and part matte painting supplied by Vernon Walker and Linwood Dunn's camera effects department. Betsy's voice-over describes her impressions of the place as Webb's 'Fort Holland theme' plays beneath. The scene is reminiscent of the opening of *Rebecca*, during which the camera moves through the closed gates towards the second Mrs de Winter's dream image of Manderley, accompanied by her voice-over. Here, looking through the gates of Fort Holland, Betsy describes the 'strangely dreamlike' garden, surrounded by a U-shaped, one-storey building, which incorporates, to the right, an ancient stone watchtower. Prominently, we're shown the statue of Saint Sebastian for the first time, the Christian martyr who, according to legend, had been shot full of arrows yet had miraculously survived – 'killed' yet resurrected, a state of being subtly echoing that of the zombie. The statue, described in the script as 'weathered and black', rests against the stone wall of the watchtower that had (presumably) once overseen the slaves working in the cane fields. Water trickles down its face, like tears. 'Combining white Christian saint and black slave, he becomes a generalized image of oppression,' observes Robin Wood.[9] The statue haunts the film, appearing in 24 shots, 9 of which feature it prominently, on each occasion reminding us of the suffering upon which Fort Holland was built.

After the garden is first seen from Betsy's perspective, the point of view switches from subjective to objective, showing images of the empty interior of Fort Holland to which

I WALKED WITH A ZOMBIE

Figure 3.3: Fort Holland.

Betsy's narration refers in the past tense as she speaks of happiness, love and madness – a shift into 'an a-chronological "descriptive syntagma" and back again'.[10] Betsy's narration for this scene wasn't scripted and was added in post-production, one of many such changes. The montage ends with a shot of Betsy's room – first empty of life then, following a lap-dissolve, showing Betsy dressing for dinner.

One could repeatedly praise Tourneur's compositions on a scene-by-scene basis; suffice to say, they are all, uniformly, excellent. Here, dusk sunlight throws the shadows of the window jalousies across the wall, like the bars of a cage – 'evok[ing] St Sebastian as a prison'[11] – another visual motif that will recur throughout the film. Betsy finishes her preparations in front of the mirror, wondering about the 'stillness of Fort Holland', then Webb's music turns subtly ominous as the shadow of a figure crosses the bars of light. Betsy pauses, uneasy, but the figure is merely the butler, Clement (Richard Abrams), announcing dinner. This fleeting moment is not in the script and was evidently conceived on the floor by Tourneur, then later punctuated by Webb's score.

Betsy leaves her room and joins Wesley Rand (James Ellison), who's waiting for her on the veranda. He introduces himself and, despite the two of them dining alone, he points out the chairs in which his half-brother Paul Holland, and his mother Mrs Rand would normally sit. It's an unusual, light-hearted moment and an efficient method for revealing the family hierarchy. Mrs Rand's chair is shown in the corner of the room in a specific cutaway shot, punctuating his statement that she's 'too wise to live under the same roof' and prefers the village dispensary. This, in turn, foreshadows the character's conflicted links to both the family and the local community. Rand turns on the charm, referring to Betsy as 'beautiful' – a word already highlighted, which will be repeated numerous times at key moments and in different contexts. Finally, when Betsy asks about the chair at the end of the table that Rand had neglected to mention, he replies awkwardly that it belongs to his brother's wife. The comment is loaded, but we won't understand why until some time later.

As the evening progresses, Rand pours himself a whisky as Betsy sips coffee. Night has fallen and, as they talk, drums begin to beat portentously in the distance. Voodoo is not mentioned but Betsy reacts with apprehension – as the viewer would be expected to do, conditioned by cinematic trope. Rand briefly plays on her fears, referring to the drums as 'mysterious, eerie', but a moment later he puts Betsy at ease. The drums are merely St Sebastian's answer to the factory whistle; the sugar syrup is about to be poured and Rand will soon have to depart to supervise it. Betsy relaxes. This is the second time a fleetingly ominous tone has been quickly punctured – Lewton and Tourneur deliberately undermining audience expectation at the same time as disabusing Betsy of the notion that the customs of St Sebastian represent a threat. The conversation switches to Holland, and Rand's jovial charm begins to fray. 'Ah, yes, our Paul. Strong and silent and very sad. Quite the Byronic character. Maybe I should cultivate it.' He's clearly jealous. A moment later Holland belatedly appears in person, casting a disapproving glance at Rand's glass of whisky. Rand, chastened, departs for the sugar mill. Holland is merely passing through to take a tray of dinner to his wife, Jessica. Curiously, Holland carries the tray to the door of the old stone tower, rather than to a room within the main building, adding to the mystery that surrounds the as-yet-unseen Jessica.

THE TOWER

Later, in her room and dressed in a black robe, Betsy prepares for bed. However, before retiring she notices something through the slats of the jalousies. From her point of view, through the window, we see Jessica (Christine Gordon) for the first time. Dressed in a flowing white nightgown she drifts eerily past the statue of Saint Sebastian and across the garden to join Holland, waiting for her beyond the open doors of the living room. She's accompanied by the first part of Webb's music cue, 'The Zombie'. In the script, this moment was followed by a scene in which Jessica attempts to play the piano – one of the rare instances in which an incident from Siodmak's discarded draft was retained and adapted – except that in Wray's version Jessica's fingers 'move strangely over the keyboard, now and again striking a hesitant note, but making no music'. The production files suggest the scene was shot but later discarded in the edit, probably owing to the similarity to a scene in *White Zombie*.

Webb's understated 'Zombie' cue continues into the subsequent sequence. We're briefly shown the statue of Saint Sebastian, accompanied by the sound of a woman sobbing somewhere off-screen. Betsy wakes and rises to investigate, heading outside and crossing the garden towards the stone tower, from which the sound originates. Inside, the tower is dark and forbidding, but Betsy is drawn onwards by continued sobbing. She warily climbs a stone staircase to the floor above, softly calling Mrs Holland's name. Pausing in a small circle of moonlight cast through a narrow window, Betsy looks back and now sees Jessica, mounting the stairs in her wake. Betsy moves forwards to greet her but then backs away, reacting fearfully to Jessica's pale, drawn face and her relentless advance, finally screaming involuntarily when she's backed up against the wall by the approaching figure. She runs across the room and Jessica follows, closing in on her again until Holland, arriving in response to the scream, calls Jessica to a halt.

The sequence is cleverly conceived and staged. It's the kind of 'horror' beat that the genre demands, yet the component parts grow out of the themes, character and narrative rather than being imposed thoughtlessly: the sobbing prompts Betsy's concerned response and, under the assumption it is her patient, motivates her sojourn to the tower; the reason behind the sobbing (Alma rather than Jessica) relates directly, as we'll learn, to one of the key themes of the film; and, finally, Jessica is not stalking Betsy

Figure 3.4: Jessica walks.

malevolently, but is merely responding, trance-like, to Betsy's call. The only 'cheat' in the scene is Maurice Seiderman's make-up for Jessica, which is noticeably more death-like than in any other scene in the film. Even this, however, can be read as Betsy's skewed perspective of reality (nothing is as it seems) in a moment of fear. We don't see a close-up of Jessica's death-mask face, even though it was scripted and evidently shot; it's likely that it was deleted in the edit, Betsy's reaction alone proving sufficient. Similarly, bats were scripted to flap around inside the tower, and animated bats were duly costed in the budget. Wisely, they were dropped by Lewton and Tourneur, probably because they smacked too much of Universal's approach to horror.

Jessica is taken downstairs by Alma (Theresa Harris) while Holland accompanies Betsy. We learn from Clement that Alma had been the source of the sobbing because 'her sister was brought a'birthing'. When Betsy and Holland depart, we linger for a moment on Clement and Alma. This is the first moment in the film (other than cutaway shots) in which action is played out that is entirely outside Betsy's point of view. Alma tells Clement that she'll stay in Jessica's room for the remainder of the night (we glean that

I WALKED WITH A ZOMBIE

Figure 3.5: History lesson.

Jessica's bedroom is accessed via a doorway within the tower) in case 'the nurse lady takes to roaming again'. Clement warns her not to go crying anymore since that's what frightened Miss Betsy, to which Alma replies: 'Well, she didn't soothe *me* any, hollering around in the tower'. It's an amusing and telling moment. Alma is not afraid to speak her mind.

Outside, in the garden, Betsy asks Holland why Alma was crying. They pause beside the statue of Saint Sebastian as Holland attempts to explain. He repeats the information given to Betsy by the coachman. 'That's where our people came from,' he tells her, 'from the misery and pain of slavery. For generations, they found life a burden. That's why they still weep when a child is born and make merry at a burial.' Holland's use of the term 'our people' could 'indicate a sense of community', writer Meaghan Walsh notes, but could equally refer to 'ownership and possession'.[12] His family, and indeed his entire estate, is forever tainted by its history, but Holland at least acknowledges the fact. Tourneur's composition here is particularly noteworthy: Holland's back appears to be pierced by the same arrow that penetrates Saint Sebastian's chest. The arrow cuts the

49

scene in a precise horizontal line, yet in other shots the angle is different, suggesting it was deliberately repositioned. It's also exactly the same arrow that's later used by Rand to 'kill' Jessica.

JESSICA

The following morning, Betsy is awoken by Alma, who reaches under the covers to wiggle her toe. Alma explains she didn't want to frighten Betsy out of her sleep, 'that's why I touched you farthest from your heart'. It's a delightfully idiosyncratic moment, yet it also suggests that Alma has been left with the impression, from the previous night's events, that Betsy is a fearful individual. Nevertheless, the two women immediately warm to each other. Like Lewton, Tourneur 'always treated Negroes with respect in his films, taking a stand against the pervasive tendency to restrict them to undignified roles'[13] and Harris's Alma is far removed from the grotesque caricatures of black servants routinely portrayed in films of that era. Betsy regards her entirely as an equal. Alma brought her breakfast on a tray, not because she's obliged to ('you don't have to do that for me', Betsy points out), but because she *wants* to. The cleverly disguised exposition that follows allows us to see, first-hand, how Alma had tended for 'Miss Jessica' prior to her sickness, serving her breakfast in bed 'with a lacy cushion to bank her head' – giving us an insight into Jessica's pampered existence at Fort Holland. Film critic Martha Nochimson notes that '[f]rom Alma's comment, we glean that "Miss Jessica" was a product of a racist milieu which caused white women to internalize their roles as passive, lovely objects'. The only perceived evil in Jessica is 'what her historical situation has made of her'.[14]

When Betsy asks about Jessica's condition, Alma replies, '[s]he was very sick and then she went mindless'. (It's interesting to note that Alma does *not* consider Jessica to be a zombie, about which, more below.) These moments of bonding between Betsy and Alma conclude with Alma presenting Betsy with a 'puff up', or *brioche*. The huge bread collapses into nothing under Betsy's fork, another visual clue that appearances can be deceptive.

Betsy's first morning on the job sees her in Holland's office, being upbraided over the events of the previous night: 'This is not a position for a frightened girl'. Betsy stands up for herself, explaining that it was something of a shock to find that her patient was 'a

I WALKED WITH A ZOMBIE

mental case'. It's a clumsy use of words that she instantly regrets, but Holland explains that his wife *is* a mental case. Betsy should remember that when 'some of the foolish people on the island start regaling you with local legends ... You'll find superstition a contagious thing.' He doesn't refer directly to either voodoo or zombies, but his words articulate another of the primary themes of the film – reason versus superstition. 'Some people let it get the better of them', Holland continues, and his final comment is more of an instruction than an observation: 'I don't think you will.' He subsequently leads her away to meet both her patient and Dr Maxwell.

Jessica's bedroom, despite being accessed via the dark tower, is brightly lit by morning sunlight, which casts shadows of the ornate, barred windows across the white walls. The script describes the room in intricate detail: 'feminine but with no suggestion of the *bagnio* [brothel]; elegant rather than seductive, reflecting a playful yet sophisticated taste'. However, the three-screen full-length mirror is a 'hallmark of great vanity'. The furniture is Biedermeier. Near the window is a harp, 'Size 22', which, along with the empty chair and curtains, gives a 'dual effect of elegance and loneliness'. Suitably, the one painting in Jessica's room is Böcklin's *Isle of the Dead*, one of Lewton's favourites since childhood. Jessica's character is defined by the objects in her room, as is *Rebecca*'s character during the scene in which Mrs Danvers shows the second Mrs de Winter her mistress's empty bedroom. It's perhaps also indicative of Jessica's character that her room is physically segregated from the rest of the building by the gloomy tower. Tourneur moves the camera around the space, blocking individual aspects at different times: the anteroom is framed first, then the camera pulls back between the drapes of Jessica's bed; next, as Betsy and Maxwell talk, it blocks out the harp (representing life) beside the window; the camera moves again into a third key position, framing Böcklin's painting (death) and the couch beneath, before returning to the room's entrance as the characters depart. As in many scenes, the actors continually cross over one another within the frame, echoing the fluidity of the camera. Webb's music cue 'Dr Maxwell' fades in as the amiable if conventional doctor (James Bell) introduces Betsy to Jessica, who's lying in bed in her trance-like state. Gone is the 'scary' make-up used for the tower scene. Maxwell states: 'She makes a beautiful zombie, doesn't she?' It's the first mention of the word in the film – excluding Betsy's opening narration – yet, Maxwell's comment isn't meant to be taken seriously. Betsy asks what exactly a zombie is, to which he scoffs, 'a ghost, the living dead

– it's also a drink'. He explains that Jessica's 'hopeless' condition is the result of a severe tropical fever that burned out 'portions of the spinal cord'. Wray's original dialogue was longer and included the words '… and certain lobes of the mind'. Some authors have commented that the explanation lacks authenticity. Nevertheless, an extreme fever, one in which the patient's temperature rises above 42°C, can indeed cause brain damage.[15] Maxwell leaves the comatose Jessica in Betsy's care – but she'll soon learn that the other members of the Holland family are as much in limbo as her patient, trapped in a situation for which each is, to some degree, culpable.

Betsy subsequently encounters Holland on the veranda, sitting as he reads a magazine (see Figure 4.3). He asks Betsy if she found her patient frightening in the daylight, teasing her mildly. She replies that Mrs Holland must have been very beautiful. 'Many people thought her beautiful', he replies sourly. His comment carries a double meaning: it implies jealousy on Holland's part that other men found her attractive, but also the unspoken suggestion that her beauty hid a darker reality beneath the surface. It's the closest he gets to criticising Jessica in the final cut of the film (about which, more below). Betsy heads on her way, but Holland can't leave the topic alone. He asks Betsy if she considers herself 'pretty' and 'charming'. When she replies that she's never given it much thought, he states bluntly: 'Don't. You'll save yourself a great deal of trouble and other people a great deal of unhappiness.' It's a mean-spirited comment, but by indirectly relating her to Jessica he's betraying the fact that he's noticed her as a woman, rather than merely a nurse. His cruelty is a cover for his real feelings.

THE VILLAGE

A fade takes us to St Sebastian's bustling village. In the background, we hear the diegetic strumming of a guitar. Betsy is on her day off, looking for 'shops and restaurants and things'. She encounters Wesley Rand, who treats her to a drink – or three – in a street-side café. In the background, we see for the first time Calypso singer Sir Lancelot, the owner of the guitar, who now begins to sing 'The British Grenadiers'. (The last four lines of this song were cut by the Irish Film Censor in July 1943, under the terms of the Emergency Powers Order that allowed the Irish government to maintain neutrality during the war.)[16] After a brief, light-hearted by-play centred around Rand's drinking, Sir

I Walked with a Zombie

Lancelot's unnamed singer begins his next song in the background – and the tone of the scene changes dramatically.

> There was a family that lived on the isle,
> Of St Sebastian a long, long while,
> The head of the family was a Holland man,
> And the younger brother his name was Rand,
> Ah, woe, Ah me,
> Shame and sorrow for the family …

Betsy tunes into it immediately. Rand tries desperately to talk over it, but Betsy wants to listen.

> The Holland man he kept in a tower,
> A wife as pretty as a big white flower,
> She saw the brother and she stole his heart,
> And that's how the badness and the trouble start …

Rand sends the café owner, Ti-Joseph (Arthur Walker), to silence the singer, but the damage has already been done. The singer duly stops – apparently unaware of Rand's proximity, though it's equally possible that his uncomfortable realisation is feigned – and announces that he'll 'creep in just like a little fox and warm myself in [Rand's] heart'. He arrives at the table with a little bow and an apology. Rand grudgingly accepts it – 'all right' – but instead of bowing out, the singer remains, adding that he has no knowledge of who made up the song. Rand tries again to dismiss him but still the singer persists in his explanation, and it's hard not to conclude that he's deliberately provoking Rand. After the singer's third expansive apology Rand finally loses his temper. Betsy calms him down, embarrassed, and Rand bemoans the fact that 'everybody' knows about the family scandal; 'Paul saw to that'. When Betsy defends Holland, the sibling rivalry again surfaces. 'He's playing the noble husband for you, isn't he? Well, that won't last long.' Betsy tries to lighten the mood, but Rand has already gulped down another rum and is growing morose. He tries to demean Holland in her eyes, as *he* has just been demeaned:

> One of these days he'll start on you, just as he did on her. 'You think life's *beautiful*, don't you, Jessica? You think you're *beautiful*, don't you, Jessica?' What he could do to

53

that word beautiful. That's Paul's great weapon, words. He uses them like other men use their fists.

Rand's comments give Betsy pause for thought because they carry the ring of truth.

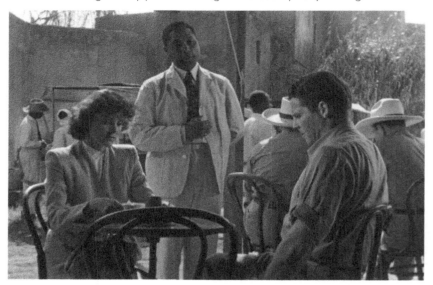

Figure 3.6: Shame and sorrow.

Night falls. Rand has drunk himself into a stupor and has passed out at the table. As Betsy tries to awaken him, the singer reappears. Slowly, menacingly, he walks towards Betsy through the shadows as he completes the song he'd begun earlier:

> The wife and the brother, they want to go,
> But the Holland man, he tell them no,
> The wife fall down and the evil came,
> And it burned her mind in the fever flame,
> Her eyes are empty and she cannot talk,
> And a nurse has come to make her walk,
> The brothers are lonely and the nurse is young,
> And now you must see that my song is sung.

I WALKED WITH A ZOMBIE

This time there's no mistaking the intentions of the singer. It's a deliberate act of defiance, finishing the song he'd been forced to abandon earlier, whilst demonstrating that his apology had been entirely insincere. Young notes that he's 'asserting his superiority over white discourse' and, via the lyrics that hint at a sexual triangle within the Holland family, reversing 'the colonial discourse of the "oversexed" native who had no respect for Western practices of monogamy'.[17] Ti-Joseph appears to be complicit, doing nothing except watch with his arms folded as Betsy backs away from the approaching singer, threatened and afraid. At this point, Edith Barrett's Mrs Rand makes her first appearance, coming to Betsy's rescue and causing the singer to quickly depart. But his point has been made. As Wood notes: 'There can't be many Hollywood movies of the early forties in which a colored character is permitted to make sly, malicious fun of whites who are neither comic nor villainous – with the film's at least partial endorsement – and get away with it.'[18]

Mrs Rand takes charge, paying the bill and having Rand sent home whilst introducing herself to Betsy. Despite Rand's drinking, he's really a 'nice boy', she insists. Nevertheless, she asks Betsy to use her influence with Holland, to have the whisky decanter taken off the table during dinner to curtail Rand's drinking. Betsy replies that she has no such influence, but Mrs Rand – who knows 'a great deal more about what goes on at the fort' than Betsy may think – insists that she does. (Notably, moments before saying that Rand is a 'nice boy', Mrs Rand had referred to Betsy as a 'nice girl'. Is she secretly hoping Betsy will fall for Rand and ease his troubles? Perhaps, though the calypso singer's hint that both Rand and Holland might vie for Betsy's affections is never properly explored in the narrative.)

TURNING POINTS

The next day, during an artfully staged scene in which the morning sun casts thin, horizontal shadows across the players, Betsy encounters Holland as he's discussing the state of the sugar cane with one of his factory workers, Bayard (Norman Mayes). Holland dismisses the suggestion that the plantation is suffering a drought, but Bayard – another who's unafraid to speak his mind – insists the cane is too dry and 'it's dangerous that way'. The dry cane is mentioned in the next scene also, though both references are hangovers from Wray's estimating draft, in which the plantation is subsequently consumed by fire.

Holland bids Betsy a good morning and says he's heard about her 'misadventure' with Wesley the night before. Betsy states she had a good time, 'up to a point', to which Holland replies that 'Wes can be very entertaining'. It's spoken without malice. Whereas Rand never misses an opportunity to talk down his half-brother, Holland never resorts to the same tactics, despite the fact Rand had tried to steal his wife; on the contrary, Holland usually turns the blame upon himself. However, when Betsy asks about removing the whisky decanter Holland appears to reject the idea, stating pointedly that he'd hired her to take care of his wife, 'not my brother', perhaps betraying a trace of envy that Wes is (briefly) the focus of Betsy's attention.

That evening, as a hot tropical breeze blows across the veranda, Betsy, Holland and Rand are midway through dinner when the distant trumpet of a conch initiates the sound of drumming. The rhythm of the drums is noticeably different to the 'factory whistle' heard previously, and Betsy asks what it means. Holland explains that the 'faithful' at the 'Houmfort' are calling on the god Damballa for rain. It's the first scene in which voodoo is explicitly mentioned. Betsy says they don't seem very disturbed by it. 'I thought voodoo was something everyone was frightened of.' Once again, audience expectation is undermined when Holland replies, with a smile, that 'it's not very frightening. They sing and dance and carry on, and then as I understand it one of the gods comes down and speaks through one of the people.' Young describes Holland's comment as 'so cynical and patronizing that the viewer begins to turn against him'.[19] His comment is indeed disparaging, but it's hard to imagine the character being any less dismissive of a Christian ceremony.

Rand reaches for the whisky decanter, only to find it missing. Holland announces that, from now on, they'll serve dinner without it. 'That's odd,' replies Rand, 'what are you trying to do, impress Miss Connell?' 'You'd make a better impression without whisky,' Holland replies smoothly. An argument brews, quickly turning to the subject of Jessica. Holland shuts down Rand with a sharp word and suggests to Betsy that she should finish her dinner in her room. She departs awkwardly, knowing that she'd inadvertently instigated the argument.

Intriguingly, the version of the scene in the shooting script had included Jessica, sitting mutely at the table during dinner. Her presence gives the written scene an entirely new dynamic, particularly towards the end when Rand accuses Holland of driving Jessica insane, pointing at her with the words, 'when you made her into *that*!' Christine Gordon was on the set throughout that day without being used, so it's not clear why she was excluded. Tourneur probably decided that the practical realities of staging weighed against it. How would Jessica eat? Would she have to be fed by someone else? Or would she not eat at all, sitting entirely immobile while the others carried on around her? The scene works perfectly well without her, but it's interesting to imagine how it *might* have played out. As things stand, Rand doesn't appear in the same frame as Jessica until seven minutes from the end of the picture – extraordinary, given his tortured obsession with her.

A lap-dissolve takes us into Betsy's room later, as she mulls over the awkward scene at dinner. The drums have stopped and piano music can now be heard in the background. A cutaway shows us that Holland is playing. The piece is Chopin's Étude Op. 10, No. 3, in E major,[20] otherwise known as 'Tristesse' – defined as a state of melancholy sadness. Betsy responds to the music, leaving her room to join Holland in the living room. Holland senses her presence and stops. As Webb's music cue 'Sympathy' begins, Betsy hovers uncertainly with her back to the door. Following the argument at dinner, she'd 'wanted to help' him, but now that she's here she doesn't know how. Holland approaches her and replies – 'with unexpected sincerity', according to the script – that she *has* helped him, and that he's sorry he ever brought her here. Betsy says she loves Fort Holland, though it's clear now that the real object of her affection is Holland himself. It's an emotional scene, made all the more moving by Webb's understated score. Despite Betsy's veiled display of affection, Holland sees nothing in himself or his situation that could possibly attract such a response. He refers to two brothers 'set against each other and a woman driven mad by her own husband'. Before Jessica was taken ill, he says, 'there was a scene. An ugly scene. I told her she couldn't go. That I'd keep her here by force if necessary.' After a pause, he continues softly, '[y]ou never knew Jessica as she was …' then trails off when he registers the sound of distant drums that have commenced again in the background. This is the third iteration of the drumming, a faster and more menacing rhythm that will be used predominantly from now onwards. The effect is immediate – 'cut[ting] between him and Betsy like a sword', according to the script – and Holland retreats into coldness and formality, effectively dismissing her from the room.

Figure 3.7: Betsy reveals her love.

In earlier drafts of the script their exchange had been longer, with Holland commenting that Jessica was 'beautiful, restless, willful – living in a world with room for nothing but her own image and her own desires'. The final shooting script had pared down some of this dialogue and the remainder was filmed but removed during editing. As noted above, Holland never (directly) speaks ill of Jessica in the final cut of the film despite doing so numerous times in the various early drafts and the shooting script. This deliberate softening of his character in the edit, to the extent that he refuses to lay blame for the family scandal on anyone except himself, allows us to warm to him more than we might have. However, by placing more emphasis on his own flaws – with the resultant implication that he *had* perhaps driven Jessica insane, as Rand alleges – the viewer's perception that he may be incapable of establishing a stable relationship with Betsy is strengthened.

Betsy is next seen walking on rocks overlooking the ocean. Despite the abrupt conclusion to the previous scene, in which Holland had 'almost thrust [her] from the room', Betsy's narration articulates her love for Holland for the first time. 'And then because I loved him I felt I had to restore [Jessica] to him, to make her what she'd been before, to make him happy.' The scene had originally been scripted to take place in front of the statue of Saint Sebastian but was shifted to the ocean during production to emphasise the romance of the moment. The day-for-night photography is made even more dream-like via a filter that creates a subtle radial distortion of the highlights gleaming on the water. Author Kyle Bishop contrasts Betsy's course of action with the path chosen by Jane Eyre when faced with the insurmountable problem of Rochester's 'mad' wife. Rather than flee 'her Thornfield', as Jane had done, Betsy 'dedicates herself to Jessica's health and recovery, selflessly hoping to bestow happiness on Holland by curing his wife'.[21] Wood notes that 'the sea is used symmetrically to mark the beginning and end of the film and the turning point of its action', and is 'invested with a specific metaphysical meaning ('deceptiveness of appearances', etc.) which has resonances throughout the film'.[22] His point is that Betsy's apparently noble decision may be driven by darker, unconscious desires, discussed below. Betsy's narration is heard here for the last time in the final cut of the film – though, as we'll see, it was originally scripted to continue through to the end.

SHOCK THERAPY

A fade takes us to a discussion between Holland, Betsy and Maxwell in Jessica's room. The mute Jessica is also present. Holland is faced with a dilemma; whether to allow Betsy and Dr Maxwell to perform insulin shock treatment on his wife in the hope of reviving her. Betsy had suggested it, though the treatment can kill as well as cure. 'Your wife isn't living … she's in a world that's empty of joy or meaning', Betsy insists. 'We have a chance to give her life back to her.'

Holland is still grappling with the decision as a lap-dissolve takes us to a night-time shot of Betsy and Maxwell at Jessica's bedside, concluding the treatment. (It appears this shot was removed from wartime UK prints by the British Board of Film Censors, because of a ban on 'operation scenes'.)[23] Betsy leaves Jessica's bedside and approaches Holland

DEVIL'S ADVOCATES

as he waits outside the bedroom doorway. She relays the news: Jessica is 'alive ... that's all'. Betsy is bitterly disappointed that she's brought him 'nothing'. Holland tells her she's brought him 'sympathy ... and a generous heart ... don't call that nothing'. As Betsy returns to her patient, Rand emerges from the black shadows of the tower behind Holland, having watched the exchange. This is another rare moment in the first half of the film that plays out beyond Betsy's point of view and earshot. 'Very sad, very sweet', says Rand maliciously. 'The noble husband and the noble nurse, comforting each other – because the patient still lives.' Clearly, he's implying that they'd *wanted* Jessica dead. While Betsy's selflessness appears to be sincere, Wood makes the point that 'the insulin shock treatment and [subsequent] visit to the Houmfort (both of which she has been assured are extremely dangerous) can be read as (unconscious) attempts to eliminate Jessica, not save her'.[24]

Figure 3.8: Better doctors at the Houmfort (Theresa Harris).

From this gloom and bitterness, a fade brings in the sound of laughter and the sight of Alma, with her friends and family, gathered around her sister's newborn baby. Betsy joins them. The group consists of Alma, Clement, Alma's sister Melise (Vivian Dandridge), her baby, Ti-Victor (six-week-old Melvin Williams), and Melise's unnamed friends (Rita

Christiani, Doris Ake, and despite best efforts, an unidentified man). Alma's earlier sorrow over Ti-Victor's birth has now given way to joy. When introduced, Betsy takes a small V-shaped enamel badge from her uniform and pins it to the baby's cardigan, so he won't ever forget that she's his friend. (The detail is unclear, but the badge looks similar to the 'V for Victory' badges worn by many people at that time – so it's possible the name 'Ti-Victor' isn't entirely coincidental.) Betsy, perhaps reacting to the sadness of the previous scene, says 'it's nice to see people so happy'. Alma replies that they're not always happy, and the conversation turns towards the inability of doctors to cure everything. She makes the comment that there are 'other doctors, better doctors', at the Houmfort.

Here, at the *exact temporal midpoint of the film*, Betsy and Alma's discussion turns towards the powers of voodoo and the possibility that a cure for Jessica could be found at the Houmfort. During the first half of the film reason had prevailed, but from this point onwards superstition increasingly governs the actions of the characters. Simultaneously, Betsy's hitherto dominant point of view – the 'eyes' of the audience and the means by which they interpret the narrative – is increasingly loosened and undermined. Not only is her voice-over absent from the second half of the film, the camera repeatedly cuts away for long periods to actions and events that Betsy cannot possibly have witnessed or even known about second-hand. As J. P. Telotte points out, '[w]ith the loss of the monological coherence initially promised by her narration, we are left with no special key to these mysteries [Jessica's condition, superstition, the power of voodoo, among other things], no comforting distance, only the inexplicable phenomena themselves, mocking our desire for explanation'.[25] It's also worth noting that the repeated use of the words 'beauty' and 'beautiful', which occur no less than 15 times during the first half of the film, vanish entirely from the second half except for one past-tense reference – as if the concept of beauty in the context of this film holds little or no meaning once superstition dominates the narrative.

Alma explains that a 'mindless' woman, Mama Rose, had been cured by the voodoo priest – or Houngan – and Betsy pointedly asks Alma if she thinks Jessica could also be cured. 'Yes, Miss Betsy, I mean that. The Houngan will speak to the rada drums and the drums will speak to Legba and Damballa.' Betsy is unsure what to make of Alma's claims and departs, mulling them over. (It's worth repeating the point that – even when discussing the 'mindless' Mama Rose and, later, Carrefour – Alma *still* doesn't entertain the notion that Jessica could be a zombie in the accepted sense of the term, adding to the ambiguity of the situation.)

In her village dispensary, we see Mrs Rand at work for the first time, rubbing ointment onto the chest of a young boy, Ti-Peter. As she replaces his shirt, she pauses, looking at the *obeah* bag that hangs around his neck. 'Ti-Peter, how do you ever expect to get to Heaven with one foot in the voodoo Houmfort and the other in the church?' This dialogue is a paraphrase of a Pastor's comment quoted in Seabrook's *The Magic Island*: 'How do you expect to limp straddle-legged into heaven with one foot in the church and the other in the *houmfort*?'[26] Mrs Rand sends Ti-Peter on his way and a change of angle now reveals that Betsy is also present in the scene. Their conversation turns to voodoo. Missionary's widow Mrs Rand talks about 'this native nonsense', states that 'these people are primitive' and berates the 'nice, level-headed girl' Betsy for asking if it has the power to cure a sick person. Mrs Rand's attitude appears to be arrogant and condescending. However, her words are hollow, a cover for the far more complex relationship she has with voodoo and superstition – and the viewer will soon find out that her comment to Ti-Peter also applies to herself. She warns Betsy against taking Jessica to the Houmfort, saying that it might be 'very dangerous' to do so, but Betsy replies – none too convincingly, given her experience in the tower – 'I'm not easily frightened'.

Throughout the first half of the film a series of 'binary oppositions' have been established that form its 'symbolic structure', tabulated by Wood as 'Canada/West Indies, white/black, science/witchcraft, Christianity/voodoo, home (Fort)/*houmfort*, harp, piano/voodoo drums' among others, stressing that these oppositions are *not* reducible to either 'good' or 'evil' and that moral certitude is deliberately undermined as the film unfolds.[27] Similarly, Michael Lee lists a series of 'doublings' resulting from the clash between the opposing systems of reason and superstition – the two zombies, Jessica and Carrefour; the fact that each resides in a fort and each walks to the other's fort; each fort has a 'doctor' who treats Jessica; and each fort houses musical instruments, 'with Fort Holland's piano doubling the Houmfort's drums and conches'.[28] In addition, Betsy increasingly takes on the mantle of Jessica as the film progresses – becoming her 'double' – and an interesting doubling of Mrs Rand and the Houmfort's Houngan is discussed further below.

I WALKED WITH A ZOMBIE

THE HOUMFORT

A lap-dissolve takes the viewer from the dispensary to the night-time garden of Fort Holland. The wind is blowing. There's no background music. The camera focuses first on Holland, seen working inside at his desk, tracks along to take in Rand, sitting drinking alone at the dinner table on the veranda, then picks up Betsy as she sneaks Jessica out of a doorway in the main building. Unseen by the others, they pass both the window of Jessica's room and the doorway into the tower, before creeping around the outside of the tower to meet Alma in the tower's *second*, previously unseen doorway. (Jessica is wearing a grey-toned dress, indicative of her 'liminal' status, neither dead nor alive, in contrast to Betsy's white nurse's uniform and a black cloak, and the black and white clothes that are worn by worshippers at the Houmfort.)[29] However, the action seen in this continuous shot raises several questions. Since Jessica's room is apparently accessed *only* via the tower, where have Betsy and Jessica been? From which room in the main building did they emerge? Why not go *directly* into the tower from Jessica's room, rather than risk being seen by traversing the garden outside? And if they did have to cross the garden for some reason, why not enter the tower via the usual doorway, rather than risk exposure by circummavigating the tower to go in via the secondary doorway? It appears the shot was designed purely for tension, rather than conforming to logic. Both Wood and Fujiwara comment at length on the stylistic importance of this tracking shot. Wood cites it as an example of 'Tourneur's style, and the natural way it associates with Lewton's taste and intelligence':

> The women's departure is shown in a camera movement that spatially connects the central characters ... As the camera turns, the two women, in distant long-shot, emerge ... and the camera follows them, still keeping its distance, as they move away from the possibility of male protection and towards the darkness ... The shot combines all the functions of long-shot/camera-movement style: it connects different lives being lived separately but simultaneously ... and by preserving physical distance, it also encourages a certain *emotional* distance. We never become identified with Betsy or her actions, hence are free to consider their implications judicially.[30]

Similarly, Fujiwara states that '[t]he shot beautifully exemplifies Tourneur's love of visual homogeneity, wholeness, and flow and his insistence on finding the simplest possible configuration of characters and themes'.[31] It's expertly staged and executed by Tourneur, setting the tone for the journey to the Houmfort that is yet to come – though it would be an injustice not to point out that the shot had been described, step-by-step, in Wray's first draft script and had been carried through subsequent drafts, unchanged, into the final shooting script.

Inside the darkness of the tower, Betsy watches as Alma scatters cornmeal on the stone floor, into which she draws a map with her finger to guide Betsy to the Houmfort. Alma warns Betsy that, at the crossroads in the cane field, she'll encounter a 'god' named Carrefour. Whether by accident or design, Harris vocalises the scripted word 'god' as 'guard'. Carrefour 'keeps the crossroads … but he won't do you no harm when he sees the voodoo patches.' Alma takes from her pocket two squares of cloth, one white and one black, which she pins to the breast of Betsy's and Jessica's clothing in turn. As she does so, a close-up on the black patch dissolves to the stark, beautiful image of Darby Jones's Carrefour, silhouetted against the night sky as he stands, immobile, in the cane field. Wood remarks: 'We don't know at this point who he is or what he is doing there; the image has a dream-like quality – inexplicable, haunting, beautiful and sinister. It creates unease without any suggestion of a shock effect.'[32] Carrefour 'embodies the links between slavery and zombies noted in Haiti by the anthropologist Wade Davis', posits author Alexander Nemerov, adding that Carrefour and Ti-Misery 'also conjure the lynching of a black man', citing anti-lynching imagery by Julius Bloch and John Steuart Curry that emphasises 'the static elongation of the black victim, turning him into an icon of suffering'.[33]

A cut takes us to Betsy, leading Jessica away from the camera between two tall rows of sugar cane. The extended sequence that follows is exquisite, arguably the finest single example of Tourneur's craft in the three films he made for Lewton, enhanced by Hunt's lighting and cinematography. It's a development of the 'Lewton walk' established in *Cat People*. Here, the sequence lasts a total of 3 minutes 14 seconds and comprises 32 cuts. Tourneur uses tracking shots extensively. Apart from the Houmfort's distant, diegetic music, heard during the last minute of the sequence, the only sounds are those of the wind blowing through the cane, and the weird 'Aeolian harp' piping of both a horse's skull and a modified gourd.

I WALKED WITH A ZOMBIE

The walk is episodic. Betsy leads Jessica forward through the cane field, following Alma's instructions, until a break in the cane, through which the bleached horse's skull is visible, indicates a divergent path. They take it. Soon after they arrive at a banyan tree on a hillock, from which hangs a dead goat. They pass it and continue as an eerie piping sound becomes audible. Betsy pauses and shines her torch ahead, and the camera tracks backwards to bring into shot a latticework of poles from which the gourd hangs. Betsy leads Jessica through it, continuing down the path and passing, next, a human skull resting within a circle of white stones on the dusty path. As Wood observes, there is a 'delicacy and simplicity' in Tourneur's direction, 'the various sinister details en route, signposting the way ... introduced without overemphasis'.[34] In the next shot the camera follows Betsy and Jessica from behind, stalking them. A conch shell is blown in the distance and Betsy pauses to look about her, tense – the camera still closing in on the back of her hair. When she moves forwards once again, pushing through the cane, we see that her white, protective voodoo patch has been dislodged. The camera closes on the patch of cloth, impaled on a cane stalk, and holds for a moment. The implication is clear: Betsy is now in trouble. In the very next shot, as her torch beam traces the path ahead, the circle of light lands on a human foot. The beam shifts quickly upwards before resting on the face of Carrefour, wearing the highly effective 'staring-eye' make-up designed by Maurice Seiderman. Betsy gasps in shock, and although the moment was designed to elicit a similar response in the audience, it can't be described as a typical Lewton 'bus', which is usually more sudden and accompanied by a sharp, loud sound. 'There is no shock-cut, no crashing chord,' says Wood, 'the *frisson* arises from the simple process of discovery, without underlining.'[35] Carrefour gazes ahead blankly, not moving, and Betsy abruptly realises that her voodoo patch is missing. She's no longer protected. Nevertheless, Carrefour remains immobile – Betsy seemingly protected by *Jessica*'s patch, still pinned to the grey dress. Betsy leads Jessica gingerly past Carrefour and continues on her way – but the camera remains on the silhouetted Carrefour a moment longer. Then, he belatedly turns and walks slowly away to his right. The staging of this moment is such that it's not immediately clear whether Carrefour is meant to be following Betsy and Jessica or merely heading away elsewhere. The geography of the 'crossroads' in the shot is confusing. (The script, however, reveals the original, equally confusing intention: Carrefour was *not* following after Betsy and Jessica but responding to a mysterious voice, inexplicably calling to him from the sugar cane, which was wisely deleted from the final cut.) Regardless, Carrefour isn't seen again in this sequence. Betsy and Jessica continue onwards towards the Houmfort.

Figure 3.9: The encounter with Carrefour.

Telotte describes the entire 'walk' sequence as 'almost an exercise in deception, since we are led to believe, by Betsy's loss of the "voodoo badge" needed to pass by Carrefour, by the recurring images of death and decay, and by the eerie sound effects, that this journey is indeed hazard filled; however, nothing happens'.[36] Similarly, Bansak states that 'this "foundless" manipulation feels like a cheat'.[37] Yet, this 'manipulation' cements the viewer's emotional identification with Betsy, underscoring the courage and determination that she's displaying whilst venturing into a world with which she's entirely unfamiliar. Plus, the sequence is entirely in keeping with the film's overall approach, consistently undercutting audience expectations.

Betsy and Jessica leave the cane fields, still following the sound of the singing, finally emerging into a clearing. The Houmfort becomes visible for the first time. As Betsy and

Jessica approach, the camera's tracking motion leaves them behind, moving in amongst the crowd of drummers and worshippers, who are singing:

> O Legba Legba marché donc,
> O Legba O Legba marché donc,
> (Solo) Papa Legba qui sortie nan la tournin,
> O Legba O marché donc,
> Marché donc Papa Legba marché donc,
> Marché donc Papa Legba marché donc,
> Papa Legba qui sortie nan la tournin,
> Marché donc.[38]

This authentic voodoo song, a summons to the god Legba, translates as 'Papa Legba walk quickly, Papa Legba has made a journey, Papa Legba walk quickly'. The attendees are dressed formally, in clean white clothes, the men wearing neckties and hats. Each wears a voodoo patch. Only one figure is dressed in black – Jieno Moxzer's Sabreur, who leads the ceremony. (The scene is based on photographs of a real Houmfort and voodoo ceremony contained in the 13 December 1937 edition of *Life* magazine.) Betsy and Jessica stand amongst the onlookers, watching nervously – but the worshippers are indifferent to their presence. As a white chicken is sacrificed off-screen at the altar, a young woman from the crowd (Jeni LeGon) steps forward with her eyes closed and joins the Sabreur's dance, seemingly possessed. The Houngan (Martin Wilkins) briefly interrupts the dance to anoint LeGon's forehead with the blood of the chicken. Soon after, she collapses and is carried away. The song to Legba finishes and the drumming grows increasingly frenzied. The Mam-Lois (Myrtle Anderson) begins the 'dance to Damballa' before Jeni LeGon returns, joined now by another woman from the crowd (Kathleen Hartsfield). They dance around the drummer (LeRoy Antoine), captured in a fluid tracking shot, before finally kneeling with their foreheads touching. The drumming builds to a climax, then abruptly eases. From the hut comes the sound of a distorted voice – seemingly that of the god Damballa – 'Where are my people? Let them bring me the rice cakes. Let them dance and be happy.'

Figure 3.10: Ceremony (Kathleen Hartsfield, LeRoy Antoine, Jeni LeGon).

The entire ceremony, choreographed by LeRoy Antoine, is a captivating *tour de force* of dancing, music, directing and cinematography. It's also treated with the utmost respect. No facet of it is sensationalised and, despite Betsy's apparent nervousness, nothing about it is remotely threatening. (The sole undercurrent of menace emerges only *after* the ceremony has concluded, when the Mam-Lois and the Sabreur take a belated interest in Jessica.) Evidently, the Houmfort sequence was originally designed to run longer. The lyrics for the Haitian song 'Le'Véé Damballa' ('Arise Damballa') were cleared for use by the Breen Office before production, and the song was subsequently recorded; yet, it doesn't feature in the final cut. Whether an extra sequence was filmed and then deleted in post-production remains unclear, but the on-screen ceremony appears to be a truncated version of the scripted scene.

As the worshippers sing 'Waléé Nan Guinin,' ('You'll Go Back To Guinée') Betsy and Jessica join the queue of people lining up to speak to Damballa. When Betsy's turn arrives, the door of the hut opens abruptly and she's pulled inside, leaving Jessica outside. In the darkness of the hut a lamp is lit – and 'Damballa' is revealed to be Mrs Rand. When

I WALKED WITH A ZOMBIE

Figure 3.11: Revelation.

Betsy recovers from her shock, Mrs Rand explains her presence. After her husband had died she'd attempted to continue the work he'd begun, but the locals had refused to take notice of her until she eventually discovered the secret of how to 'deal with them'. For example, she'd repeatedly begged a new mother to boil the drinking water for the sake of her child, but the woman only listened when Mrs Rand couched the instruction in different terms: the god Shango would kill the evil spirits in the water if she boiled it. The deception worked. Ever since, Mrs Rand has been masquerading as Damballa to dispense medical wisdom to the Houmfort worshippers. Wood asks: 'Is she Christianizing voodoo or voodooizing Christianity?'[39] As Young explains, there's no clear answer:

> At first glance it would seem that Mrs Rand's point of view – western science and rational thinking, a little bit of 'practical psychology' – is being privileged. However ... her discourse is questioned. Perhaps the greatest evidence that the white point of view has been subverted, is Mrs Rand's final belief [revealed in a later scene] that it was she who precipitated Jessica's ... lapse into zombiism.[40]

Meanwhile, outside, Jessica's trance-like demeanour has drawn the attention of the Mam-Lois and the Sabreur. The Sabreur approaches Jessica, slowly and menacingly – then plunges the sword into her arm (carefully staged to address instructions from the Breen Office to avoid 'unacceptable gruesomeness').[41] Jessica doesn't flinch, nor does she bleed. Several of the worshippers mutter the word 'zombie'. Once again – and with increasing frequency as her narrative point of view is progressively abandoned – Betsy doesn't witness this moment but is nevertheless made aware of it by the sounds emanating from outside the hut. Concerned, Mrs Rand tells Betsy to get Jessica back to Fort Holland. Betsy quickly departs with Jessica as the Houngan instructs the worshippers to 'let them go'. A single, long, fluid, tracking shot – from the banyan tree, through rows of cane – illustrates Betsy and Jessica's urgent retreat to Fort Holland.

CONSEQUENCES

Betsy creeps out of the tower, having returned Jessica to her room, and heads across the garden to her own room. But Holland is waiting for her. When he asks where she's been, she confesses. 'I wanted to help you', she says, in a direct echo of the scene in which her love for Holland had first become evident. 'There's no telling what you may have started with this insanity', he says sharply, before immediately softening and asking, 'because you wanted to give my wife back to me? Why should that mean so much to you?' (The transition from hard to soft is somewhat abrupt, the result of dialogue being deleted during editing. In the full exchange, Holland accuses Betsy of endangering Jessica's life and demanding to know why she had done it – a further example of Holland's character being rendered less harsh during cutting.) In response, Betsy replies: 'You know why. You saw it the other night, at the piano.' Her comment is subtly punctuated by Webb as his music cue, 'Return from the Houmfort', segues briefly into Chopin's 'Tristesse'. Holland confirms that he could 'hardly believe' what he'd seen – 'a woman who had compassion for me, who loved me'. Here, we venture directly into *Rebecca* territory, specifically the key scene in which de Winter finally disabuses his second wife of the notion that he'd loved Rebecca. In *Zombie*'s 12 October script the dynamic had been identical, as was Holland's line of dialogue: 'I hated her'. In the script he went on to say that Jessica's selfishness made her 'empty and dead' and that she was 'a beautiful possession to own and hold' but that he'd never had 'a moment's peace or happiness with her'. However, in subsequent page revisions, and in the final cut, the point is made far less directly. 'You think I loved Jessica and want her back. It's like you to think that. Clean, decent thinking.' After a pause, he adds, 'I only wish it were true'. As Webb's music is replaced by the diegetic sound of the voodoo drums, a sense of ominous anticipation accompanies the transition to the next scene.

The next morning, beside the statue of Saint Sebastian, Betsy joins Alma who is holding the reins of the horse belonging to a visitor – the island's Commissioner, Jeffries – whilst simultaneously trying to eavesdrop on a group conversation that is taking place inside. This scene was a late addition that allowed Lewton to delete from the script a long, dialogue-heavy and static scene in which Jeffries, Holland, Rand, Maxwell and Mrs Rand discussed the trouble brewing at the Houmfort because of Betsy's visit with Jessica. Instead, the discussion is merely observed by Betsy and Alma from a distance, with the results reported in a later scene. Nevertheless, Alma has gleaned enough from their body language to know that the topic is 'something very bad' – a point stressed by the subsequent series of scenes that intercut between Fort Holland and the Houmfort.

A lap-dissolve takes us to the figure of a blonde-haired doll being dressed in a tiny costume that is a miniature version of Jessica's nightgown – echoing the words of Alma, who'd earlier said that the morning routine with Jessica was 'just like dressing a great big doll'. As the camera tracks back we see we're in the Houmfort at night, and that the (voodoo) doll is in the hands of the Sabreur. Ardel Wray recalled her involvement with this scene:

> I particularly remember that doll because Val sent me out to find and buy one 'cheap' ... That was another thing about Val – a low budget was a challenge to him, a spur to inventiveness, and everyone around him caught the fever. Anyway, I got a rather bland-faced doll at a department store, cheap, and by the time she had been dressed in a soft grey robe, and her hair had been combed out to the appropriate 'lost girl' look, she, too, was somehow transformed.[42]

On the Warner DVD commentary, Steve Jones expresses his 'disappointment' with the doll, saying it looks 'remarkably like a Barbie doll'.[43] However, in a film in which audience expectation is routinely undermined, a more 'traditional' voodoo doll – for example, made out of wax – would have seemed too much of a cliché. The choice of doll was deliberate on Lewton's part, the script describing it as 'a cheaply-made bisque [porcelain] doll' and a 'little five-and-ten-cent store doll'. Nevertheless, Jones and Newman also compliment Lewton for his refusal to explain to the audience through exposition how voodoo dolls are supposed to work. Lewton rarely, if ever, underestimated the intelligence of his audience.

In the revised, final shooting script, this scene is accompanied by Betsy's voice-over narration:

> It had been foolish of me to take my patient to the Voodoo ceremony. The sight of her … seemed to set alight blazing fires of superstition and curiosity. I don't think anything else was talked about for days. Even among the house servants at Fort Holland – people who had known and cared for Mrs Holland – there was wild talk. I even heard that ridiculous word – Zombie –

This narration was ultimately deemed redundant and excised during post-production, but it's indicative of the original intention to carry Betsy's voice-over through to the end of the film. From this point onwards, events move irrevocably beyond Betsy's control.

Back at Fort Holland, as Betsy pulls the covers over the sleeping Jessica and drops the net curtains around her bed, she's joined by Holland. He explains that Jeffries and Maxwell are 'in a great stew about … those people at the Houmfort' who won't stop drumming until they get Jessica back to 'finish their ritual tests'. A decision has been made to send Jessica away to the island of St Thomas, to the asylum. (Appropriately, St Thomas – a real island in the Caribbean – is named after Thomas the Apostle, who doubted that Jesus had been raised from the dead.) It's also made clear that Rand had repeated the accusation that Holland had deliberately driven Jessica insane. As he speaks, Holland symbolically turns away from Betsy, the camera panning with him until he's framed in front of Jessica's mirror – but he's unable to escape his entanglement with Betsy since her reflected image is now in front of him once more. The reflection departs as Betsy joins him in person. The camera angle shifts again, to a two-shot with Böcklin's *Isle of the Dead* in the background, almost looming over them. Betsy insists that Rand's accusations cannot possibly be true, but the conflicted Holland has 'gone over it and over it' and is no longer sure.

At this point, a lengthy continuation of the scene was deleted in post-production, during which Holland forcefully denounced Jessica and described the sequence of events on the night she fell ill. The excised dialogue reveals that Holland had been 'raging and nagging at her; piercing her vanity', because Jessica was 'cold and selfish – without any warmth of generous life in her'. Betsy insists that a mere quarrel couldn't have driven Jessica insane, but Holland reveals she'd subsequently collapsed, displaying no sign of a pulse, heartbeat or breathing. He and Rand were frightened and sent for Maxwell, but it took the doctor over an hour to arrive, during which Jessica 'came out of her coma and began to babble in delirium – raging with fever'. However, this premature revelation – that Jessica had fallen into a coma – would have undercut a later revelation, examined below, had it not been removed.

Cut to the Houmfort. Carrefour, eyes staring blankly, is framed holding the Jessica doll in his hand, the scene lit by flickering firelight (see Figure 2.3). The Sabreur glides slowly into the frame and closes Carrefour's fingers around the doll. After a moment he takes the doll from Carrefour and steps backwards, urging Carrefour to follow. Carrefour once again takes the doll, and once again the Sabreur takes it from him and steps back. Carrefour approaches and grips the doll for the third time. The entire scene is silent except for the rapid beat of the drums, yet the intention behind these actions is abundantly clear. It ends exactly as it had begun, with Carrefour alone in the frame, holding the doll.

In the garden at Fort Holland, Holland insists that Betsy must return to Canada, still blaming himself for Jessica's condition. 'Since you've been here I've seen how fine and sweet things could be between a man and a woman', he says, finally returning the affirmation of love that Betsy had revealed earlier. However, '[i]t's no good for you to stay so long as I have this fear of myself'. She rests her head on his chest and he holds her – their first physical embrace.

Betsy subsequently spends the night in Jessica's room, to watch over her patient. Betsy is seen asleep in the background, on the couch beneath the Böcklin painting, the shadow cast by the bars on the window cutting across the shot. In the foreground is the harp. A breeze shifts the filmy curtains and they play briefly and magically across the strings. Michael Lee cites this as another example of the 'doubling' of musical instruments

Figure 3.12: Carrefour walks.

between Fort Holland and the Houmfort. '[A] primitive Aeolian flute made from a gourd is both heard and seen during Jessica's walk to the Houmfort … and a breeze transform's Jessica's harp into an Aeolian harp.'[44] Following a brief cutaway to the garden outside – a shot of a shadow crossing the footpath – Carrefour's silhouette is cast across the wall over the sleeping Betsy. Betsy wakes and rises, quickly checking on Jessica before picking up a nightgown from a chair at the end of Jessica's bed and heading out to trace the source of the shuffling sound. Observant viewers will note that the dressing gown belongs to Jessica – a fact confirmed by the script – and by donning Jessica's mantle, Betsy's conversion into the 'double' of Holland's 'absent' wife is complete. This action soon places her in (apparent) jeopardy.

Betsy creeps into the garden, passing the statue of Saint Sebastian, in a sequence that might be described as a 'mini-Lewton walk'. She advances silently and cautiously. She's first distracted by the sound of a frog croaking as it jumps into the small pond at the foot of the statue – then startled by the twitter of an owl and looks up sharply. It's the closest we get to a Lewton 'bus' in this film. Now, however, she sees the door of the tower opening and she retreats into the cover of the foliage. She again hears the sound of shuffling feet and sees Carrefour's shadow crossing the path. Afraid, she hurries to Holland's bedroom door, trying unsuccessfully to open it whilst calling his name. Holland responds immediately and, together, they watch as Carrefour walks towards them along the veranda – the zombie now coming for Betsy in the mistaken belief, because of the dressing gown, that *she* is Jessica. Holland shouts at Carrefour to stop but he continues his relentless approach, reaching out his hands. As his face looms so close to the camera lens that it goes out of focus, a voice abruptly calls from off-screen, halting him in his tracks. This is the second time Betsy has been 'stalked' in this manner – first by Jessica in the tower – and each time the 'zombie' is stopped by a character calling them by name. The source of the voice this time is Mrs Rand, who orders Carrefour to 'go back'. The zombie complies. (One might wonder how it is that Mrs Rand has power over Carrefour, but her ambiguous position within the hierarchy of the Houmfort offers an explanation – a conclusion strengthened by the revelations contained in the next scene.) This is the last in a series of incidents that '*suggest* some threat which never materializes'.[45] Betsy's encounter with Jessica in the tower, the approach of the calypso singer, the walk to the Houmfort during which Betsy lost her protective cloth patch, her 'dangerous' visit to the Houmfort itself – in each case the supposed 'threat' leads to no tangible harm, further stressing the key theme of the deceptiveness of appearances.

The next morning, Holland informs his mother that Betsy is leaving the island. However, Mrs Rand's expressions of regret are interrupted by the arrival of Rand and Dr Maxwell, bearing 'unpleasant news'. There is to be a 'legal investigation' as a result of Rand's accusations and the fact that one of the 'voodoo people' had entered Fort Holland the night before. Rand says angrily that the investigation can be avoided if Holland admits that he's responsible for Jessica's condition. At this point, Mrs Rand has heard enough. She steps forward, anguished, and says that she can explain everything to the commissioner. She confesses that *she* is responsible for turning Jessica into a zombie, whilst 'possessed' during a ceremony at the Houmfort. It had happened after the 'ugly scene' that Holland alluded to earlier. 'I went to the Houmfort', Mrs Rand says. 'I kept seeing [Jessica's] face, smiling because she was beautiful enough to take my family in her hands and tear it apart ... and asked [the Houngan] to make her a zombie.' When she'd returned to Fort Holland that night she'd found Jessica raging with fever.

In truth, Mrs Rand's belief that the Houngan made Jessica a zombie at her request doesn't square with the mystified reaction that Jessica had elicited at the Houmfort. However, perhaps she hasn't fully grasped the consequences of entering into their ceremonies. Since she was, in her own words, possessed, it's possible she subconsciously committed the act of zombification *herself* – her hatred of Jessica manifesting itself in tangible form through sheer willpower, projecting her destructive id much like Dr Morbius in *Forbidden Planet* (1956) more than a decade later. This would far better explain the Sabreur's confusion about Jessica's state of being and the fact that the Houngan is seen aiding him in his quest for answers.

Figure 3.13: Confession.

Either way, Mrs Rand's confession articulates for the first time the possibility that Jessica's condition was caused by magic rather than illness. It lends weight to the assumption that her trance-like state is unnatural. From this point onwards, the viewer must juggle two opposing explanations. Dr Maxwell scoffs at Mrs Rand's words. For a person to become a zombie they must first die, but he doesn't remember Jessica dying, 'or even being in a state resembling death. No coma, nothing.' (As mentioned above, the deletion of Holland's earlier dialogue allows the audience to accept Maxwell's 'no coma' comment at face value – at least, for the time being.) His scientific explanation of Jessica's illness appears to convince Mrs Rand that she's wrong. Confused and saddened, she heads upstairs. The camera follows her. Holland and Rand are in the foreground, and just before the two of them pass out of frame as the camera pans, Rand places his hand on Holland's shoulder. It's a fleeting moment, possibly missed by many viewers since the eye is drawn to Mrs Rand in the upper half of the frame – yet it indicates a significant shift in the relationship between the two brothers. From this point on, Rand no longer blames Holland for Jessica's condition. He *believes* his mother.

The intercutting between the Houmfort and Fort Holland continues. Having failed in his attempt to have Carrefour abduct Jessica, the Sabreur resorts to other forms of magic. The doll representing Jessica is placed on the ground attached to a long thread, the other end of which is held by the Houngan, crouched inside the hut. The Sabreur straddles the thread, acting out a pantomime of pulling it. The doll begins to move slowly towards him.

A cut to Fort Holland shows Jessica seemingly responding to the Sabreur's actions. She walks out of the tower and approaches the open gate, stopping only when Betsy closes the gate, blocking her path. (At the Houmfort, the doll also stops, despite the continued urging of the Sabreur.) Rand joins Betsy and Holland (thereby sharing the frame with Jessica for the first time), saying that the Houmfort is 'trying to get her back … they have charms that can draw a man halfway around the world'. Holland says it's 'all nonsense'. However, Rand, convinced by his mother's confession, points out that Maxwell was wrong – Jessica *had* fallen into a coma before the doctor's arrival. At that moment, the drumming from the Houmfort ceases, apparently releasing Jessica from its influence. Betsy leads her back inside.

Following a transitional shot of the statue of Saint Sebastian, Betsy crosses the garden to return to her room. She finds Rand sitting nearby, deep in troubled thought. 'She ought to be free', says Rand of Jessica. 'You could do it, Betsy. You're a nurse, you have the drugs.' Betsy refuses. 'Her heart beats. She breathes. That's life, Wes. I once took an oath to guard life.' Rand apologises for asking, but insists 'she's already dead'. When he then points out that Jessica's continued existence stands in the way of Betsy and Holland's happiness, she cuts him off a second time. Rand finally turns away and Betsy enters her room.

This is the last dialogue exchange in the film. The remaining four and a half minutes of the film play out entirely through Tourneur's visuals, and the only voice heard is the one belonging to the mysterious narrator at the close. The scene ends with a curious diagonal black wipe, unlike any other transition in the film. It follows Betsy from left to right as she enters the doorway to her room. The reason it was chosen over a fade or a lap-dissolve can only be guessed at, but it perhaps symbolises the end of Betsy's direct involvement in the narrative: her final decisive action is to refuse Rand's request to euthanise Jessica, and she takes no further part in the film's climax except as an observer during the final scene. It's yet another example of Lewton's unconventional approach to narrative, since the active involvement of the central protagonist in a story's resolution is usually a given. When queried on the similar unusual ending to Lewton's *The Ghost Ship*, director Mark Robson had this to say:

> These were unstructured works. Unstructured in the sense that character conflicts between protagonist and antagonist were diffuse ... In many ways they broke many of the rules of storytelling ... Their form is different from any films of that period or since – they're much freer. They follow very few dramaturgical rules.[46]

Betsy has been left in an intractable situation. Despite her best efforts – above and beyond her duty of care – she's been unable to cure Jessica. An affair with Holland, for a woman of her character, is out of the question. Assuming the same laws apply to St Sebastian as to the New York of *Cat People*, Holland is forbidden to divorce an 'insane' spouse, just as Irena's husband was unable to divorce her. And, finally, Betsy's morals and Hippocratic oath rule out the possibility of ending Jessica's suffering. Betsy has no choice but to step back from any further course of action. Nevertheless, up to this point, she is the only character in the film who has attempted to confront and change the status quo, and by taking Jessica to the Houmfort she'd already set in motion 'the entire chain of subsequent actions to the end of the film'.[47]

ENDINGS

Rand sits at a table with his head in his hands, alone, the whisky bottle and a glass beside him. He looks up and sees Jessica leave the tower once again and walk towards the gate. She stops, unable to progress. Rand watches her for a moment. At the Houmfort, the Sabreur is still trying to coax movement from the Jessica doll but, unable to do so, he turns to the Houngan and whispers in his ear. Cut back to Fort Holland. Rand rises from the table, walks off the veranda and opens the gate to allow Jessica to leave. His demeanour is subtly trance-like, suggesting he may be acting under the influence of voodoo. Having watched Jessica depart, he turns to the statue of Saint Sebastian. He pulls out one of the arrows that pierce the statue, then follows after Jessica. Lap-dissolve to the Houmfort, where the Sabreur now crouches over the doll. He waves his hand and the doll falls forwards onto its face. Then he takes out a long steel needle and plunges it downwards into the back of the doll. At that instant, the drumming stops.

On the beach, Jessica lies sprawled on the sand. Rand kneels over her, his back to the viewer, slowly rising with the arrow still in his hand. Jessica's head and upper torso are hidden from us, but the implication is clear: 'Whether he was impelled by enchantment or was simply the victim of his own dark imaginings upon abandoning the rational world, we never learn', states Telotte.[48] Wood insists that Rand's actions 'are subconsciously induced by voodoo'.[49] Young concludes:

> No rational solutions are offered to the audience, thus adding layers of complexity to the film's meaning. If it is indeed voodoo that killed her, and this is not so implausible given the film's general tolerance in the matter, then it again affirms the subversion of white discourse and power. Effectively the black 'inferiors' have reduced their white masters to dolls, taking life from them as they please.[50]

Nevertheless, if voodoo *was* guiding Rand's hand as he struck down Jessica, it shouldn't necessarily be seen as an act of spite. It was possibly an act of mercy, to put Jessica out of her misery – a view shared by Nochimson, who asks: 'Is this the way the descendants of the slaves take their revenge, or is it an act of compassion to purge the Hollands of their demons?'[51] Conversely, if we take the view that Rand was solely in control and that no voodoo was involved, the action can be seen as a *dual* act of mercy on his part: freeing the woman he loves from her limbo, but also freeing Holland and Betsy to be together in recompense for the blame he'd repeatedly laid upon his half-brother.

DEVIL'S ADVOCATES

Figure 3.14: Consumed by the sea.

After a moment of silence following Jessica's (second?) death, Webb's music cue 'End Title' begins to infiltrate. Rand sees Carrefour approaching from the shadows. In response, he gathers Jessica up in his arms and walks down towards the rough sea. Carrefour follows him. Rand backs away into the ocean, deeper and deeper. Carrefour pauses at the edge of the waves, watching as Rand and Jessica are consumed. The final shot, a down-angle on Carrefour as a wave breaks behind him, is singled out by Nemerov as an iconic image 'that makes Carrefour a far more tragic figure than the two white people who disappear into the sea'.[52] The subsequent lap-dissolve to the next scene is a dissolve-within-a-dissolve – and the same wave is seen breaking behind Carrefour *twice*. The reasoning behind this is most likely mundane – the usable part of the outgoing shot wasn't long enough to sustain for the duration of the scene transition, so it was repeated – but it's a testament to the beauty of Tourneur's imagery that it was engineered to remain visible for as long as possible.

The lap-dissolve takes us to the dead face of Jessica, floating in calm water, followed by a further transition to a group of flounder fishermen wading, knee-deep, in a dead calm sea. As they work by torchlight, 'O Marie Congo' is again heard on the soundtrack, although judging by the fishermen's lack of lip movement the singing does not appear, on this occasion, to be diegetic. Inevitably, they find Jessica's body. As they retrieve her, an alternate voice-over is heard for the first time. Never scripted, it was added by Lewton in post-production. It picks up the narration that Betsy had seemingly abandoned and, in place of the judgemental comments that had been deleted from Holland's dialogue, passes the final verdict on Jessica's character:

> O, Lord God most holy, deliver them from the bitter pains of eternal death. The woman was a wicked woman, and she was dead in her own life. Yea, Lord, dead in the selfishness of her spirit. And the man followed her. Her steps led him down to evil, her feet took hold on death. Forgive him, O Lord, who knowest the secret of all hearts. Yea, Lord, pity them who are dead. And give peace and happiness to the living.

The voice-over continues across the final shots of the film, which show the fishermen carrying Rand's body back into Fort Holland through the gate, passing the statue of Saint Sebastian. Following behind them is Carrefour, holding Jessica's body. Betsy and Holland watch solemnly whilst Mrs Rand weeps. As the narrator begins his final sentence, '... give peace and happiness to the living', Betsy is shown in Holland's arms, her face resting on his chest. The shot, however, in 'no way guarantees [their] happiness: as Betsy and Jessica are frequently paralleled in the film, we are free to believe that Betsy's fate will be similar to that of her deceased patient'.[53] The film's final shot, as Webb's music builds to a climax, is a tracking shot that closes in on the statue of Saint Sebastian, holding for a moment before a lap-dissolve to the RKO exit logo.

The second narrator's voice, and the meaning behind it, has been a source of much speculation. 'This final solemn "say" comes from a mysterious, never identified speaker', states Telotte.[54] Sylvie Pierre concludes that the voice is 'a kind of non-person beyond the actors, the epilogue being entrusted to the purely musical closure of an impersonal incantation'.[55] A more interesting analysis comes from author André Solnikkar, who posits that the disembodied voice is that of Saint Sebastian/Ti-Misery himself, a 'timeless, passive, wise observer' of the events at Fort Holland who was in a position to pass moral judgement on Jessica.[56] This theory is given weight by the presence of the statue on-screen during the latter part of the voice-over. However, an equally interesting conclusion can be drawn from the fact that the voice we hear is almost certainly that of the Houngan, whom we heard ordering the worshippers at the Houmfort to allow Betsy and Jessica to depart: the intonations of his voice are identical. (Actor Martin Wilkins' voice was dubbed – his natural voice had a higher pitch – so the linking of the Houngan's voice to the final narration during post-production, provided by actor Jess Lee Brooks, appears to have been a deliberate choice.) Since he's evidently calling upon the Christian God in this narration, it raises the possibility that the Houngan has appropriated as much of the Christian faith as Mrs Rand has appropriated the voodoo faith – another interesting 'doubling' of the two characters.

Telotte observed:

> [B]racketing the story with such varied voices violates the usual voice-over approach which ... relies on a single narrator to present or comment upon the events ... By violating these expectations, however, the film produces an element of complexity seldom met with either in genre programmers or in more traditional film forms.[57]

Whilst this is true, it's possible that Betsy *does* have the final word after all – though not in the conventional sense – if one now returns to the narratively dislocated opening shot of the film which, at face value, can only have taken place *after* the conclusion of the story. Could Betsy's walk on the beach with Carrefour hint at a more hopeful future for the island and its inhabitants?

Either way, the final on-screen image is that of Saint Sebastian/Ti Misery, representing both Christian martyr and black slave. As with the final narration, the selection of this shot was made during post-production, and the ending described in the shooting script – which had indeed been shot by Tourneur – was deleted. The closing scene went through an interesting evolution at script stage that's worth tracing briefly. In Wray's estimating script, the closing sequence consisted of an elaborate charade organised by Holland. Feigning indifference, but 'with a twinkle in his eye', Holland appears to deliberately avoid Betsy as she prepares her final departure from Fort Holland. But as Alma and Clement accompany her to the gate, she sees that Holland is waiting for her beside the horse and trap that is to take her to the boat. To her delight, he's going with her on her journey. In the final shooting script, the end scene had shifted to Canada, neatly 'book-ending' the film with the snow-bound setting of the Parrish & Burden Sugar

I WALKED WITH A ZOMBIE

Company. Here, Betsy is seen waiting outside the building, looking 'very attractive and very happy', and her scripted closing narration reads as follows:

> It was a sad time at Fort Holland. Mother Rand was completely broken by the tragedy. But she's a woman of courage. She's begun to build up her life again at St Sebastian – It's a good life and a full one. As for Paul and me – it wasn't a simple problem for either of us.

Holland then exits the building and takes Betsy's arm. He apologises for keeping her waiting: 'Invoices and stock lists', he explains. Betsy reminds him they're dining with friends, and she wouldn't want it said that 'the Hollands are always late'. They walk away arm in arm, evidently married and contented.

Figure 3.15: The deleted end scene: Betsy and Paul Holland in Canada. © 1943 RKO Pictures, Inc.

This conventional 'happy' ending was ultimately deemed far too pat for Lewton's taste, blunting the themes that had been carefully woven through the narrative. Instead, we end on the tearful face of Saint Sebastian, which reminds us that, whilst we may wish for 'peace and happiness', the past will always remain to haunt us. The audience is sent from the theatre, not with a bromide, but with a resonating image of human suffering.

SUMMATION

Faced with a lurid title and subject matter imposed by the studio, Lewton 'could justifiably have employed a conventional horror formula'.[58] Instead, he and his unit pursued an approach even more radical than that deployed for *Cat People*. A story rich in ambiguity and thematic resonances was conceived, then continually revised and refined throughout the development, production and post-production processes – surely in the knowledge that something extra special was being created – far beyond the care and attention normally invested in low-budget genre fare. The end result was a haunting and elegiac female gothic thriller in the tradition of *Rebecca*, sufficient to satisfy the expectations of both the RKO front office and a general audience, but simultaneously delivering a bold meditation on slavery and oppression. The fact that Lewton had to dodge the censors and the propagandists along the way makes the achievement all the more impressive.

For those who seek them, there are no clear answers to the questions raised by the narrative, which 'attempts to find a reality that lies somewhere in the intersection of [a] Venn diagram of all the facets and aspects presented'.[59] Is Jessica a zombie? Is her condition a result of natural illness, the overbearing oppression of her husband or voodoo magic? Should we believe Mrs Rand's confession? Were Betsy's actions driven by unconscious desires less noble than they appeared on the surface? Was Rand acting under the influence of outside forces when he killed Jessica, or his own will? Can Betsy and Holland ever find happiness together? The audience is left to draw its own conclusions.

It's perhaps instructive to apply to *Zombie* a similar test to the one Lewton and Bodeen had applied to *Cat People*: does the story still work if one dismisses the horror and supernatural elements? The answer is, yes – though that entails a couple of difficulties. For example, how to explain Carrefour's condition? It appears he's a 'genuine' zombie, though equally he could be suffering the same syndrome as the 'mindless' Mama Rose, described by Alma. The fact that Jessica doesn't bleed, according to the witnesses at the Houmfort, is slightly more problematic. We can take Betsy's word that Jessica 'breathes … her heart beats', so a rationalist can take comfort in the fact that puncture wounds sometimes bleed internally more than externally. Beyond that, it's easy to see

Dr Maxwell reeling off an obscure 'scientific' explanation. Finally, the apparent cause-and-effect implied by the intercutting between Fort Holland and the Houmfort during the 'voodoo' sequences could be taken as coincidence – Jessica drawn from her room merely by the sound of music (the drums), and Rand acting entirely under his own volition. However, a supernatural explanation is there for those who choose to accept it. Despite the ambiguity, the film remains dramatically satisfying – a rare achievement.

Just as there are no simple answers to the narrative questions, there is no single, glib 'message'. Instead, the film is layered with numerous interlinked themes and subtexts that the viewer is invited, consciously or subconsciously, to contemplate. Just as the beauty of the island hides the pain and suffering of the past, Jessica's beauty is said to disguise the selfishness of her spirit. Jessica's 'evil' is a symptom of the social environment in which she was raised, defined by the colonial attitudes of the past. The limbo into which she has been cast, 'empty of joy and meaning', is the state of being of the zombie, which, in turn, represents the hellish, never-ending torment of slavery. This oppression is represented by the statue of Ti-Misery/Saint Sebastian, which also represents the Christian religion of the slave-trading nations, a religion whose missionary widow resorts to voodoo ... and so on. The complex, overlapping links continue, eventually coming full circle.

Yet no such analytical deconstruction can ever prove entirely satisfactory, since the whole is unquestionably greater than its component narrative, thematic and visual parts. Like any work of art, it engages the viewer on an emotional level that defies comprehensive description. Ultimately, as Robin Wood observed, *I Walked with a Zombie* works 'by means of poetic suggestiveness rather than of clearly definable meaning'.[60]

Notes

1. Dannis Peary, 'Mark Robson Remembers RKO, Welles & Val Lewton', *Velvet Light Trap* 10 (1973), 35.
2. *I Walked with a Zombie*, estimating script, 30 September 1942, RKO Radio Pictures Records (Collection PASC 3). UCLA Library Special Collections, Charles E. Young Research Library, University of California, Los Angeles.
3. *Motion Picture Herald*, 20 March 1943.

DEVIL'S ADVOCATES

4. *Collins English Dictionary* (HarperCollins, 1998), 214.
5. Unless otherwise indicated, all quotes are taken from the revised final script, 24 October 1942, RKO Records.
6. Correspondence, *I Walked with a Zombie*, Production Code Administration Records, Margaret Herrick Library, Los Angeles, California.
7. Gwenda Young, 'The Cinema of Difference: Jacques Tourneur, Race and I Walked with a Zombie (1943)', *Irish Journal of American Studies* 7 (1998), 110–111.
8. J. P. Telotte, *Dreams of Darkness: Fantasy and the Films of Val Lewton* (University of Illinois Press, 1985), 47.
9. Robin Wood, 'Notes for a Reading of I Walked with a Zombie', *Cineaction!* 3/4 (1986), 20.
10. Wood, 'Notes for a Reading of I Walked with a Zombie', 15.
11. Martha P. Nochimson, 'Val Lewton at RKO: The Social Dimensions of Horror', *Cineaste* 31/4 (2006), 11.
12. Meaghan Walsh, 'Survivors and Victims: Gothic Feminism, Deconstruction and Colonialism in I Walked with a Zombie' (MA diss., Savannah College of Art and Design, 2008), 14.
13. Robin Wood, 'The Shadow Worlds of Jacques Tourneur', *Film Comment* 8/2 (1972), 69.
14. Nochimson, 'Val Lewton at RKO', 11.
15. Medlineplus, accessed on 27 March 2023, https://medlineplus.gov/ency/article/003090.htm.
16. Irish Film Censor's Records, Trinity College Dublin, accessed on 6 January 2022, https://www.tcd.ie/irishfilm/censor/show.php?fid=3452.
17. Young, 'The Cinema of Difference', 112.
18. Wood, 'The Shadow Worlds of Jacques Tourneur', 69.
19. Young, 'The Cinema of Difference', 113.
20. Michael Lee, *Music in the Horror Films of Val Lewton* (Edinburgh University Press, 2022), 51.
21. Kyle William Bishop, *American Zombie Gothic: The Rise and Fall (and Rise) of the Walking Dead in Popular Culture* (McFarland, 2010), 84.
22. Wood, 'Notes for a Reading of I Walked with a Zombie', 19.
23. Correspondence, *The Ghost Ship*, Production Code Administration Records.
24. Wood, 'Notes for a Reading of I Walked with a Zombie', 20.
25. Telotte, *Dreams of Darkness*, 52.
26. W. B. Seabrook, *The Magic Island* (Literary Guild of America, 1929), 107.
27. Wood, 'Notes for a Reading of I Walked with a Zombie', 20.
28. Michael Lee, 'Sound and Uncertainty in the Horror Films of the Lewton Unit', in James Wierzbicki (ed.), *Music, Sound and Filmmakers* (Taylor & Francis, 2012), 115.
29. Bishop, *American Zombie Gothic*, 88.
30. Wood, 'The Shadow Worlds of Jacques Tourneur', 69.
31. Chris Fujiwara, *Jacques Tourneur: The Cinema of Nightfall* (McFarland, 2011), 94–95.
32. Wood, 'The Shadow Worlds of Jacques Tourneur', 69.

33. Alexander Nemerov, *Icons of Grief: Val Lewton's Home Front Pictures* (University of California Press, 2005), 104.
34. Wood, 'The Shadow Worlds of Jacques Tourneur', 69.
35. Wood, 'The Shadow Worlds of Jacques Tourneur', 69.
36. Telotte, *Dreams of Darkness*, 52.
37. Edmund G. Bansak, *Fearing the Dark: The Val Lewton Career* (McFarland, 2003), 153.
38. Correspondence, *I Walked with a Zombie*, Production Code Administration Records.
39. Wood, 'The Shadow Worlds of Jacques Tourneur', 70.
40. Young, 'The Cinema of Difference', 110.
41. Correspondence, *I Walked with a Zombie*, Production Code Administration Records.
42. Joel E. Siegel, *Val Lewton: The Reality of Terror* (Secker & Warburg, 1972), 41.
43. Steve Jones and Kim Newman commentary, *I Walked with a Zombie* (Warner, 2005), DVD.
44. Lee, 'Sound and Uncertainty in the Horror Films of the Lewton Unit', 115.
45. Telotte, *Dreams of Darkness*, 52.
46. Peary, 'Mark Robson Remembers RKO, Welles & Val Lewton', 37.
47. Wood, 'Notes for a Reading of I Walked with a Zombie', 16.
48. Telotte, *Dreams of Darkness*, 54–55.
49. Wood, 'The Shadow Worlds of Jacques Tourneur', 70.
50. Young, 'The Cinema of Difference', 113–114.
51. Nochimson, 'Val Lewton at RKO', 12.
52. Nemerov, *Icons of Grief*, 126.
53. Wood, 'Notes for a Reading of I Walked with a Zombie', 20.
54. Telotte, *Dreams of Darkness*, 44.
55. Clare Johnston and Paul Willemen, *Jacques Tourneur* (Edinburgh Film Festival, 1975), 47.
56. Correspondence with author André Solnikkar, 6 January 2022.
57. Telotte, *Dreams of Darkness*, 44.
58. Telotte, *Dreams of Darkness*, 43.
59. Walsh, 'Survivors and Victims', 8.
60. Wood, 'The Shadow Worlds of Jacques Tourneur', 70.

Chapter 4: 'Most Smashing Sleeper of the Season'

By the time production wrapped on *Zombie*, the chronically insecure Lewton, who'd been buoyed by the *Cat People* preview in October, had received further encouraging news. Trade showings of the earlier film had been run the previous week, resulting in largely positive reviews. Lewton must have been particularly pleased with *The Hollywood Reporter*'s observation that he had created 'something fresh and new in the psychological "horror" field'.[1] Even though *Cat People* had yet to prove its worth in front of a mainstream paying audience – the sternest test of all – the trade feedback would have fortified Lewton during *Zombie*'s editing process, resulting in the bold and significant post-production adjustments outlined in Chapter Three. Nevertheless, *Zombie* still faced several hurdles. It first had to secure the approval of his RKO bosses, then satisfy the PCA, and finally, pass muster with the LA Board of Review.

Figure 4.1: Rand contemplates setting Jessica free.

Opinions were gathered from RKO staff about the merits of the picture, and several of these internal 'preview' reports survive in the studio archive. Reactions ranged from 'good' to 'excellent', with two people rating it as superior to *Cat People*. One accurately described it as '*Rebecca* in a West Indies voodoo setting', praising the film as a 'first-rate psychological melodrama', with Tom Conway singled out as being 'another Lawrence [sic] Olivier'. Most considered it entertaining, with good box-office potential. Only one staff member, from the publicity department, felt that it was 'strictly for horror film fans', and that there was 'a little too much of the psychological and not quite enough of sheer horror'. He nevertheless conceded that it packed some 'swell suspense and chills'.[2]

Lewton received a further boost to his confidence on 14 December – perhaps the most personally rewarding of all – in a telegram from David O. Selznick, who'd viewed *Cat People* for the first time the previous evening. Selznick was 'very proud' of Lewton, stating that the film 'at one stroke establishes you as a producer of great competence and I know of no man in recent years who has made so much of so little as a first picture ... in no way does it look like a "B" picture, and it is worthy of important presentation'. Selznick concluded by saying that he'd sent a copy of the telegram to 'Mr Koerner, who I am sure feels as I do, that RKO is fortunate to have made such a ten strike as the acquisition of your services as a producer'.[3] Coming from a giant of the industry, the wire surely laid to rest any lingering doubts amongst RKO's front office staff regarding Lewton's abilities.

RKO formally signed off on *Zombie*'s title on 16 December – not that any alternative title had been considered – and, two days later, the Breen Office reviewed the film. Lewton had already addressed most of their concerns during script revisions, and they raised no objections to the filmed content. However, by this time the OWI was exerting pressure on RKO to view the film, and they potentially stood in the way of *Zombie* being granted an export licence.

HIDE AND SEEK

As outlined in Chapter Two, the OWI had been engaged in a battle of wills with the studios throughout the summer of 1942 over its efforts to regulate the story content of the studios' pictures. By late October, just as *Zombie* was going into production, the OWI had grown so frustrated by studio resistance that the chief of the OWI's

Hollywood Office, Lowell Mellett, decided they must urgently 'bolster OWI's clout' through indirect means.[4] His strategy was to establish a close liaison with Watterson Rothaker's LA Board of Review, which had the power to refuse the export of motion pictures. If Mellett could garner Rothaker's support in denying licences to films to which the OWI objected, they could effectively strong-arm the studios into complying with their instructions, on penalty of losing foreign box-office takings.

The plan was put into effect in mid-November, whilst *Zombie* was still in production. A representative of the OWI's Overseas Branch, Ulric Bell, joined Mellett in Hollywood. This 'man from Overseas', Mellett reasoned, 'could more credibly and subtly carry OWI's objections to Rothaker'.[5] Simultaneously, Mellett began to play hardball with the industry. On 9 December, he sent shockwaves through the studios with a stern letter which effectively demanded that *all* scripts should be sent to his office for review, that all films should be viewed at the 'long cut' stage and that all studio contact with the armed forces and foreign governments should be channelled through his office. It was a risky strategy that backfired. The industry fought back and, with the exception of Warner Brothers, 'lined up in solid opposition to Mellett's demand'.[6]

All this had played out in the background whilst *I Walked with a Zombie* was in post-production and, soon after, Bell began pestering RKO to show him *Zombie*. *Cat People* had been reviewed by the OWI in mid-November and found to have 'no major or minor war content'.[7] However, given the OWI's desire to micromanage the representation of black people on screen – and particularly their insistence that the issue of slavery be avoided at all costs – *Zombie* was an entirely different matter.

Bell's attempts to influence the LA Board of Review were bolstered on 11 December when a revised code was sent to Rothaker from the Office of Censorship. Previously, Rothaker had been permitted to bar the export of films *only* on the grounds that they contained scenes or information of direct military value to the enemy. Now, however, his remit had been extended to a range of issues, some of which covered the portrayal of American society.[8] Aware of the danger, Lewton and RKO deliberately stalled Bell, repeatedly making excuses throughout December and January that *Zombie* was not yet ready to be viewed. Quite how they managed to get away with this isn't clear, especially since the PCA had seen the completed film in mid-December, but it's likely that the furious reaction from the studios to Mellett's December letter provided adequate and convenient cover.

That Rothaker was under considerable pressure from Bell is evidenced by a request Rothaker made to the Breen Office in late January, asking for written confirmation that they saw 'no reason why the RKO-Radio picture titled I WALKED WITH A ZOMBIE should not be exported to Latin America'.[9] The Breen Office complied – possibly because of Lewton's cordial relations with Breen himself – and, armed with this support, Rothaker was able to hold firm against Bell. Only *after* Rothaker had issued the export licence did RKO finally allow the OWI to view the film, on 3 February 1943. Bell was furious. He'd tried for 'six weeks' to get a look at the film, and accused RKO, amongst other studios, of playing a 'hide-and-seek race … to get the censor's okay before they show their stuff to OWI'.[10]

Figure 4.2: The Houmfort.

Although it came too late to make a difference, the OWI's analysis of the film makes for interesting reading. Judging by their report, it appears the nuances of the story were lost on the reviewers. For example, their accusation that the dialogue in the film presents the black characters as 'primitive' and 'superstitious' is grossly disingenuous, given the fact that comments of this kind, made by screen characters with hidden agendas, are subsequently undercut later in the narrative. Similarly, the reviewer's statement that there are 'no cultured or educated Negroes in the story' is simply not true, Sir Lancelot's character being an obvious case in point. The report concludes with the statement that 'it is probable that the Overseas Branch of OWI will judge this picture to be unsuitable for release in certain parts of the world'.[11] Bell subsequently (and belatedly) wrote to Rothaker on 10 March 1943, despite the film having already 'escaped' the OWI's purview. He wrote that *Zombie* is 'an unfortunate picture from the war information standpoint', and that its net effect is to 'draw a sharp line of cleavage between the two peoples [white and black]'. He added that the film 'should not be exported and is potentially very bad for domestic distribution'. However, the quality of the film had not escaped his attention and he concluded the memo with the following comment (magnanimous under the circumstances): 'It must be said, however, that with the material it used, RKO made a special effort to handle carefully and with good taste the situations involving white and blacks'.[12]

Bell continued his campaign to influence the Office of Censorship and finally took complete control of the OWI's Hollywood office in July 1943. By that time, Rothaker had fallen into line and now 'followed [Bell's] recommendations in almost all cases'.[13] Had *Zombie* been produced just a few months later, it would doubtless have been refused export. Not only that, it might never have been made in the first place, since it would have been financial madness for a studio to make a film 'known in advance to be doomed to domestic exhibition exclusively'.[14]

PROMOTION AND RELEASE

While RKO played 'hide-and-seek' with the OWI, the publicity department had been preparing *Zombie's* forthcoming exploitation campaign. *Cat People* – which had finally opened in December, immediately proving a hit – had been marketed as a 'Romantic Mystery Thriller', highlighting the term 'Love and Superstition' to indicate key elements of the narrative, with a slant designed to appeal to a female audience.[15] The *Zombie* campaign now doubled down on *Cat People's* winning strategy.

Zombie's press book repeatedly emphasised the link between horror and romance, using phrases such as 'witchcraft and superstition blended with an absorbing romantic theme', 'Voodooism and romance', 'Strange Tale of Romance and Thrills' and 'Horror and Romance in New Thrill Film'.[16] The front cover, primarily monochrome but with the text highlighted in garish green, was dominated by the image of Jessica – the 'monster' deemed by the publicity department to be the most exploitable element – her eyes blank and without pupils, her arms outstretched, while the faces of Betsy, Holland and Rand were relegated to the lower-left corner. Female imagery also dominated the posters and promotional press photographs (unlike the 1956 rerelease posters, which featured Carrefour prominently). The ambiguity of the narrative was cast aside for the poster taglines, which suggested that Jessica was indeed a zombie: 'Dead yet alive!' and a 'Blonde Beauty – doomed to be one of the walking dead'.

Figure 4.3: The nurse discusses her patient.

Zombie's promotion, according to author Tim Snelson, 'appears to directly interpellate the home-front woman', citing another poster tagline, 'imagine yourself perhaps hungering for love – dying for just one warm kiss … yet alone in a world of people …

a part of, yet apart from, everyone you hold dear'. Referencing Diane Waldman's discussion of film promotion during that period – which suggests that female audiences in particular were expected to identify with situations presented by a film's narrative in relation to their own lives – Snelson posits that *Zombie*'s advertising 'was playing upon the wartime mood of emotional limbo' at a time when 'boyfriends, husbands, and potential dates [were] either fighting overseas … or relocated for war work'. He also notes that the press book 'highlights the links between the character of the trained nurse Betsy and the actress who portrays her, Francis Dee', who'd undertaken 'courses in Red Cross nursing – a contribution to the war effort shared by over three million other women'.[17]

With the mobilisation of women for war work, theatres saw an increase in the percentage of female patrons making up the audience – and a significant increase in the numbers of women attending *horror* films, a phenomenon that Snelson examines in depth. There's nothing in the RKO records that indicates the exact composition of the audiences for Lewton's first two features, but given the story content and the promotional strategy it would be logical to conclude that women were heavily represented. More generally, Lewton summed up why, in his view, horror became so popular during the early 1940s:

> People are worried. There's a war, and whether they know it or not, they're scared. It's a very real fright – and a horror picture can be the antidote. They can sit in a theatre and look at a story that's fantastic … and shudder and groan and tremble just as if it were real. It gives us an outlet, a means to sublimate fear.[18]

Trade showings of the film were run on 15 and 16 March 1943. That same week, it was previewed at the Hawaii Theatre in Hollywood. The reviews were mixed. *The Hollywood Reporter* (on 16 March) rated it highly, predicting that it stood 'an excellent chance of breaking the records that "Cat People" broke. In many respects, it is a smoother entertainment.' The *Motion Picture Herald* concurred (on 20 March), citing it as 'an exceptionally well made production' with 'many ingredients … calculated to tingle the spine'. However, these were balanced by several poor reviews. *The Film Daily*, for example, (on 17 March) found it 'lacking in action'. It went on to say that '[e]ven devotees of horror films … will find it tough to extract more than a passing amount of entertainment' since 'not very much happens, nor much that is of any great interest'. On the same day, *Variety* stated that the film 'fails to measure up to the horrific title'. The acting came in for particular criticism: 'With few exceptions, [the] cast walks through the picture almost as dazed as the zombies'. Overall, the proceedings were judged to be 'inanimate'.

Nevertheless, Lewton took comfort from the fact that many doubtful critics had been proved wrong in their initial assessments of *Cat People*, which was still raking in excellent box office – to the extent that the planned release dates of both *Zombie* and *The Leopard Man* were pushed back. 'Record-breaking playing time throughout the country on RKO's "Cat People", including numerous holdovers and extra bookings, has caused postponement of national release dates on … [the] second and third respectively in the new series of psychological horror films', announced *The Hollywood Reporter* on 18 March. Such was the demand for *Cat People* that 'RKO has switched from renting it out to theatres for a flat fee – as was usual for B pictures – to a percentage of the box-office take usually reserved for A features'.[19] In a bold move, RKO took the same approach with *Zombie* from the start of its run.[20]

Meanwhile, ignoring the fact that Inez Wallace's screen story hadn't, in the end, formed the basis of the film (see Chapter Two), RKO selected Cleveland, Wallace's home town, to host the world premiere of the film. It seems no expense was spared. RKO head of exploitation Terry Turner, along with his field staff and the head of advertising and publicity, S. Barret McCormick, masterminded the campaign. A total of 71 radio spot announcements were run across 3 local stations during an 8-day period in the run-up to the opening, accompanied by 'exceptional coverage by the local newspapers with considerable art and feature stories, in addition to a large scale advertising schedule'.[21] As might be expected, *The Cleveland Plain Dealer*, the newspaper for which Wallace worked, was at the forefront of the promotion. Three days in advance, despite a sprained ankle that had left him on crutches, Tom Conway made the train journey from Los Angeles to Ohio, according to *The Hollywood Reporter*.[22] On the afternoon of Wednesday, 7 April 1943, RKO branch manager Bernard Kranze entertained Conway, Christine Gordon and Wallace at a 'cocktail party' attended by 'newspaper representatives, leading exhibitors and city officials'.[23] Later that evening, as midnight approached, Gordon donned a fluorescent costume and walked 'several blocks' from her hotel to the Allen Theatre, 'followed by a mobile radio unit which broadcast a description of the sensation she created among the pedestrians by her ghostly appearance'. Arriving at the theatre itself, she was met by a 'remarkably effective' marquee display 'which involved the use of four zombie figures reclining in coffins. At intervals these figures, bathed in eerie light, sat up in their coffins and emitted terrifying shrieks.'[24] The stars were in attendance at the start of this unusual 'midnight to dawn' premiere, and a press photograph from that night shows Wallace, flanked by Conway and Gordon and surrounded by a packed crowd, being interviewed at the entrance to the theatre by Sidney Adorn of radio station WGAR.

The carefully orchestrated campaign paid off, with *The Hollywood Reporter* recording that the film 'is breaking all house records including the first day mark'.[25] However, the premiere prompted a particularly spiteful review from the Montreal *Gazette*, titled 'Cleveland Views Local Girl's Film'. After stating that the presence of 'Miss Wallace … and even the mayor' would not be sufficient reason for attending, the unnamed (and perhaps jealous) journalist went on to say: 'We should like to see the [preview] cards commenting on Miss Wallace's effort, both from her fellow workers and from her confreres on rival Cleveland papers. It would only be embarrassing if Miss Wallace had delusions of artistic achievement.'[26] Nevertheless, *Variety* confirmed *Zombie* as the '[m]ost smashing sleeper of the season', stating that it was 'the biggest hit the Allen [theatre] has had since *Pride of the Yankees*'.[27]

Two weeks later, on 21 April, the film opened at the Rialto in New York. *The Daily News* gave it a moderately positive review, but Thomas M. Pryor in *The New York Times* was not remotely impressed. After reporting that the film opened to:

> a packed house … and, at one point, drew a horrified scream from a woman patron, [Pryor opined that] to this spectator, at least, it proved to be a dull, disgusting exaggeration of an unhealthy, abnormal concept of life. [Noting that the PCA had protested the use of] such expressions as "hell" and "damn" in purposeful dramas like "In Which we Serve" … then how much more important is its duty to safeguard the youth of the land from the sort of stuff and nonsense their minds will absorb from viewing "I Walked with a Zombie"???[28]

The review was inexplicably harsh: of the negative reviews elsewhere, none of the reactions equated to the 'disgust' claimed by Pryor. Even the Catholic Legion of Decency (which later found Lewton's *The Seventh Victim* objectionable) rated *Zombie* as 'unobjectionable for adults'.[29] Snelson notes that the 'combination of bemusement and ferocity ... with which the reviewer pulls rank with his superior cultural capital over an assumed deluded mass is atypically extreme for a *New York Times* horror film review', adding that Pryor 'revealingly cites the film's transgressive ideological positioning in relation to the war'. After referring to the OWI's wartime motion picture directives, Snelson concludes:

> It is not surprising, then, that *I Walked with a Zombie*, with its evocation of America's and Britain's imperialism, and particularly their shameful histories of slavery, might be perceived by *The New York Times* as incompatible with Hollywood's promotion of the democratic ideals for which the allies were fighting. Although America's history (and present) of racial domination was a pervasive absence in most wartime films, Lewton managed to sneak through a film that provoked questions about American race and gender relations under the guise of a lurid horror shocker.[30]

It's worth noting that *The New York Times*, on more than one occasion, had sided with the OWI in criticising Hollywood,[31] and in-house critic Bosley Crowther seemed to harbour a particular grudge against *Zombie* even though he hadn't actually reviewed the film, commenting later in a generic piece about horror films that 'a daub such as "I Walked with a Zombie" drains all one's respect for ambulant ghosts'.[32] In any event, Pryor's review either had no impact or, perhaps, backfired. Soon after, *The Hollywood Reporter* announced that the film 'closed a two week run ... at the Rialto theatre with a gross take estimated as 25 per cent more than its record-breaking predecessor, "The Cat People"'.[33]

Nine days after the New York opening, on 30 April, *Zombie* opened nationwide to an excellent box-office response. According to *The Hollywood Reporter* (on 7 September), when *Zombie* finally opened in Los Angeles at the Hawaii Theatre, paired with Lewton's third film *The Leopard Man*, the double bill established a new opening-day record, beating by $21.00 the previous record holder, *Citizen Kane*. There were, however, a few exceptions to *Zombie*'s overall popularity. A theatre manager in South Dakota, with

I Walked with a Zombie

a 'small town patronage', wrote: 'In the picture the nurse walked with a Zombie. The patrons walked out of the theatre, and the exhibitor walked around in circles trying to think what to do to make up for the loss.'[34] Similarly, a manager in Scotia, California ('small lumber town patronage') reported 'many walkouts and complaints', and noted that the picture seemed 'a complete waste of supposedly scarce film'.[35] Evidently, the film played better in metropolitan areas than elsewhere.

Overall, however, *Zombie*'s popularity continued to grow. Oscar Shepard in the *Bangor Daily News* observed that most horror films were 'plain moronic' but *Zombie* was 'so artistic' that it deserved particular attention:

> When Frankenstein has one of his periodic resurrections, children in the audience (and it's very hard to fool them with synthetic thrills) just laugh a little – like the New York critics. But yesterday afternoon, at the Bijou, we sat near a group of youngsters who were all but frightened out of a year's growth. For that matter, there were several times when a wave of nervous tension swept through the entire audience. No, this picture is not moronic; it is adult, it is intelligent, it has dialogue that is really clever.[36]

Even *Parents* magazine noted the film's merits. Their 'Family Movie Guide' described it as a 'de luxe horror film – that is, it depends for its effects not on sensationalism but on good story telling, intelligent direction, believable acting and appropriate, but not over emphasized, background music'. Whilst they suggested it was not suitable for young children, they rated it as 'good' for adults, and appropriate for youths if they were 'used to films of this sort'.[37]

BRITISH RELEASE

The Breen Office's concerns that the film would be denied a release in the UK, owing to a supposed blanket ban on 'horror' films, proved groundless. The film was awarded an 'A Certificate' by the British Board of Film Censors (BBFC), meaning that patrons under the age of 11 could only be admitted in the company of a parent or guardian. The BBFC file relating to the film appears to have been destroyed in the late 1950s – part of a clear-out of pre-1957 files to make space – but the limited amount of information on the BBFC's (occasionally inaccurate) website suggests it was cleared for exhibition on

14 May 1943. However, the website's claim that no cuts had been necessary is open to question. At least two old prints of the film – one still used by the BBC as of this date, and a different print used for the 4-Front Video 1998 UK VHS release – reveal a cut of approximately ten seconds made to the 'operation' scene, as outlined in Chapter Three. Either way, trade showings of the film began on 22 June and the film went on general UK release on 6 September.

Figure 4.4: A resonant image of human suffering.

Once again, reviews were mixed. *Kinematograph Weekly*'s review (on 24 June 1943) found it 'a little too far-fetched to thrill intelligent audiences and yet not exciting enough to chill the spines of the masses', but that it had 'catch-penny potentialities for industrial halls'. Reviewer K. F. B. in *The Monthly Film Bulletin* praised the technical aspects of the production, stating that the team of Lewton and Tourneur 'again achieves here a telling mixture of sound normality and the occult', and that the film is 'workmanlike and at times imaginative'. However, while noting that '[a]lmost all the weird sounds and strange happenings are traced to reasonable causes', K. F. B. couldn't resist imposing a moral judgement by questioning 'whether it is right to perpetuate and strengthen superstition by proving the efficacy of magic'.[38] *The Cinema's* C. A. W. stated that there is 'little narrative interest in so fantastic a line up of confected thrill and sensation', but for 'the appropriate patron there is strong melodrama'. In addition, 'tribute may be paid to the restrained directorial treatment, the effectively eerie backgrounds and the competence of the leading characterisations'.[39] C. A. Lejeune's review in *The Observer* was brief but fairly complimentary:

> Something special for the photographic connoisseur and the student of oddities. A chilly story of Haitian voodoo, perfunctorily acted, but endued with an insinuating atmosphere by the man behind the camera.[40]

VINDICATION

Zombie's exact foreign distribution pattern isn't known, but a search of various international newspaper archives indicates that, during the wartime years at least, the film was shown in the following countries and regions: Latin America, Canada, Australia, New Zealand, the UK, Ireland, India, Palestine, Sweden and Turkey.[41] The US box-office returns carried *Zombie*'s gross to within touching distance of *Cat People*'s domestic take, even though less money had been spent, overall, on promotion. The film fared less well overseas, resulting in the combined worldwide gross falling just short of the total that had been achieved by its predecessor. (Contrary to oft-repeated but wildly erroneous estimates, which claimed *Cat People* grossed up to $4,000,000, the actual figure was $1,200,000.)[42] Nevertheless, because of the lower expenditure on prints and advertising, after deductions *Zombie* ended up on par with *Cat People* in terms of studio profit. Final dollar tallies in the RKO records are contradictory, with one source suggesting *Zombie* took the crown by the wafer-thin margin of approximately $3,000,[43] whilst a second, perhaps more complete tally, made *Cat People* more profitable by a margin of approximately $2,000.[44] In the context of a give-or-take million-dollar box-office gross for each picture, the films effectively ended neck-and-neck.

Lewton's gamble had paid off handsomely, proving that he wasn't merely a one-hit wonder. However, it came at a cost. A week after *Zombie*'s February preview, whilst Lewton was in production on *The Leopard Man* and simultaneously preparing the final script for *The Seventh Victim*, he wrote to his mother and sister that '[t]here was hardly a night since Christmas that I got home before midnight. For the first time in my life I'm really tired.'[45] The strain of his obsessive approach to producing was beginning to take its toll. In addition, once the front office realised that Lewton's new 'horror' formula was paying dividends, RKO placed even greater demands on his services, picking up the option on his contract ahead of the scheduled renewal date and now expecting him to make 'more and more pictures – six next year', instead of the four contracted for his first year. 'If I have to do this I'll either be dead, insane, or out of the business in two years', he wrote. In a revealing comment indicative of his frame of mind at the time, he continued, 'I know so surely that whatever small talent I have in this field will be broken and ruined by working in cheap things'.[46] Lewton protested that RKO was working him too hard and, soon after, he engaged the services of agent Myron Selznick (brother of David) to 'clear matters up for me ... relieve me of some of the pressure and get me one or two decent [non-horror] pictures to do'.[47] Evidently, Selznick was able to achieve this, since Lewton's production roll-call for 1943–44 was reduced to four pictures, two of which were non-horror films. Nevertheless, the intensity and devotion that Lewton poured into each successive production never slackened and he eventually drove himself to a heart attack, in November 1945, at the age of 41.

Lewton returned to work in January 1946, but the premature death of Charles Koerner a month later – the producer's most stalwart supporter at RKO – effectively brought about the end of his tenure at the studio. He accepted an offer from Paramount later that same year, inviting select members of his RKO unit to follow him – most notably Ardel Wray, writer Josef Mischel and his personal assistant Verna de Mots – but he never again found the creative freedom he'd enjoyed under Koerner. His attempts to develop films of interest were stifled by studio politics and interference. Ardel Wray noted that Lewton 'played studio politics like a Renaissance courtier and, so it seems to me, didn't have the slightest comprehension of the way that the grubby game was really played'.[48] He produced one forgettable film for Paramount, *My Own True Love* (1948), and another, *Please Believe Me* (1950), for MGM. His final film, the underrated *Apache Drums* (1951) for Universal, saw a return to Lewton's old form, but he died soon after – in March 1951, at the age of 46 – having effectively worked himself to death.

However, in the immediate wake of *Cat People* and *Zombie*, his radical approach to screen horror had begun to exert an influence on genre films released by rival studios.

Notes

1. *Hollywood Reporter*, 13 November 1942.
2. Production files, *I Walked with a Zombie*, RKO Radio Pictures Records (Collection PASC 3). UCLA Library Special Collections, Charles E. Young Research Library, University of California, Los Angeles.
3. Telegram from David O. Selznick to Val Lewton dated 14 December 1942, The Val Lewton Papers, Manuscript Division, Library of Congress, Washington, DC.
4. Clayton R. Koppes and Gregory D. Black. *Hollywood Goes to War: How Politics, Profits and Propaganda Shaped World War II Movies* (University of California Press, 1990), 80.
5. Koppes and Black, *Hollywood Goes to War*, 106.
6. Koppes and Black, *Hollywood Goes to War*, 109.
7. OWI Report, *Cat People*, Records of the Office of War Information, Record Group 208; National Archives at College Park, College Park, MD.
8. Koppes and Black, *Hollywood Goes to War*, 125.
9. Correspondence, *I Walked with a Zombie*, Production Code Administration Records, Margaret Herrick Library, Los Angeles, California.
10. Koppes and Black, *Hollywood Goes to War*, 127.
11. OWI Report, *I Walked with a Zombie*.
12. Memo from Bell to Rothaker dated 10 March 1943, OWI Report, *I Walked with a Zombie*.
13. Koppes and Black, *Hollywood Goes to War*, 140.
14. *Motion Picture Herald*, 14 August 1943
15. *Cat People* press book.
16. *I Walked with a Zombie* press book.
17. Tim Snelson, *Phantom Ladies: Hollywood Horror and the Home Front* (Rutgers University Press, 2014), 36–39.
18. *Bristol News Bulletin*, 9 October 1942.
19. Undated letter established as 8 February 1943, The Val Lewton Papers.
20. *Hollywood Reporter*, 2 February 1943.
21. *Showman's Trade Review*, 24 April 1943.
22. *Hollywood Reporter*, 6 April 1942.
23. *Showman's Trade Review*, 17 April 1943.
24. *Showman's Trade Review*, 24 April 1943.
25. *Hollywood Reporter*, 13 April 1943.

26. *Gazette,* Montreal, 20 April 1943.
27. *Variety,* 14 April 1943.
28. *New York Times,* 22 April 1943.
29. *Exhibitor,* 2 March 1943.
30. Snelson, *Phantom Ladies,* 41–42.
31. Koppes and Black, *Hollywood Goes to War,* 105.
32. *New York Times,* 13 June 1943.
33. *Hollywood Reporter,* 10 May 1943.
34. *Motion Picture Herald,* 18 December 1943.
35. *Motion Picture Herald,* 6 November 1943.
36. *Bangor Daily News,* 1 July 1943.
37. *Parents,* 18 April 1943.
38. *Monthly Film Bulletin* 10/115, July 1943.
39. *Cinema,* 23 June 1943.
40. *Observer,* 5 September 1943.
41. Online research courtesy of author André Solnikkar.
42. *Variety,* 5 January 1944.
43. Richard B. Jewell, 'A History of RKO Radio Pictures, Incorporated, 1928–1942' (PhD thesis, University of Southern California, 1978).
44. Richard B. Jewell, 'RKO Film Grosses, 1929–1951: The C. J. Tevlin Ledger', *Historical Journal of Film, Radio and Television* 14/1 (1994), 37–49.
45. Undated letter, established as 8 February 1943, The Val Lewton Papers.
46. Undated letter, established as 8 February 1943, The Val Lewton Papers.
47. Undated letter, *circa* March 1943, The Val Lewton Papers.
48. Joel E. Siegel, *Val Lewton: The Reality of Terror* (Secker & Warburg, 1972), 92.

Chapter 5: Legacy

The box-office success of *I Walked with a Zombie* confirmed the viability of Lewton's radical approach to screen horror and cemented his position at the studio. Its primary legacy, therefore, was the continuation of his cycle of films – and, more importantly, the continued freedom to shape the stories in the way he saw fit. Lewton made nine more features for RKO between 1943 and 1946, giving directors Mark Robson and Robert Wise their first feature credits in the process, and whilst the box-office returns varied, each film sought to push the boundaries of the form in some way.

The Leopard Man (1943) and *The Seventh Victim* (1943) – although superficially the detective-type films requested in Lewton's initial four-film contract – were both radical departures from the norm in terms of style and narrative concerns. The former employed an experimental structure, focusing on one character after another in its thematic exploration of destiny, whilst the latter is an utterly unique study of 'resignation and despair, the perpetual awareness of death at the very centre of life'.[1] They were followed by *The Ghost Ship* (1943), a meditation on authority and madness, and *Curse of the Cat People* (1944), the inevitable sequel demanded by RKO, which emerged as a delicate exploration of child psychology. Lewton broke from the thriller/horror mould with *Youth Runs Wild* (1944), a look at wartime juvenile delinquency, and *Mademoiselle Fifi* (1944), a subtle condemnation of France's Vichy administration, adapted from two stories by Guy de Maupassant. However, poor box office for these latter films resulted in RKO pressing Lewton to produce three more horror films, starring Boris Karloff. Initially suspicious of Karloff owing to his long association with Universal's horror films, Lewton soon formed a close friendship with the actor, who'd grown tired of formulaic genre fare and who warmly embraced Lewton's tasteful and intelligent approach. Their collaboration produced three period-based films: *Isle of the Dead* (1945), which returned to the theme of reason versus superstition explored in *Zombie*; *The Body Snatcher* (1945), an adaptation of Robert Louis Stevenson's classic tale, considered in some quarters the finest horror film of the 1940s; and *Bedlam* (1946), set in London's St Mary of Bethlehem hospital for the insane and based on the eighteenth century illustrations of William Hogarth. Lewton's eleven RKO films form a body of work with a unique signature that has grown in stature ever since.

WIDER INFLUENCES

Despite the acclaim, many early authors and historians of the genre were of the view that the Lewton films were so exceptional, they were 'in some ways outside the mainstream development of the horror film' and 'had little direct influence on its evolution'.[2] They were perceived as a stylistic cul-de-sac, 'chamber music against the seedy bombast of the claw and fang epics of the day'[3] that changed the genre only 'for a brief time'.[4] More recently, however, the influence they exerted on the horror genre and beyond has undergone a reappraisal. The restrictive definitions of genre in 1940s Hollywood cinema are gradually breaking down (see, for example, *Rediscovering 1940s Horror Cinema: Traces of a Lost Decade* by Mario DeGiglio-Bellemere, Charlie Ellbé and Kristopher Woofter), replaced by an appreciation of the cross-fertilization that took place during this 'era of tremendous creative ferment'.[5]

Although Lewton's films are often excluded from the history of *film noir* – probably because they're perceived as horror movies – a strong case can be made that they 'are equally at home in the film noir genre', and that '[a]ll of his films – whether with elements of the horror piece, mystery, or period film – are marked by the same visual style and sense of fatalism that was so noteworthy in the noir film'.[6] Indeed, given their dates, the early Lewton films arguably influenced the development of the genre itself. Author Rick Worland states that Lewton's films demonstrate 'the clearest link between 1930s horror and 1940s Film Noir'.[7] Edmund Bansak concurs, stating that 'a surprising number of noir elements were already present in the horror genre', and that '[t]he Lewton RKO films have strong associations with the early 1940s examples of noir melodrama, which is what sets them apart from the horror fare of the previous decade'.[8] Author Dale Ewing cites *I Walked with a Zombie* and *Cat People* specifically as horror films from which 'film noir gained a mise-en-scène of repulsion and dread'.[9]

Similarly, the early Lewton films are linked to the development of the female gothic genre in cinema. Author Helen Hanson places *I Walked with a Zombie* fourth in a chronological list of 27 films which she defines as the 'Female Gothic Cycle of the 1940s',[10] and Tim Snelson traces a direct line of influence between *Cat People*, *Zombie* and later films on Hanson's list (see below).

Focusing on the horror genre itself, author Ian Olney posits that a number of post-war horror films – made in the 'lost' decade of horror between 1946–1956 – 'treat gender in an unconventional, even radical, fashion, positioning women as their protagonists and pitting them against male monsters in stories that could be described as feminist', acknowledging that Lewton's films anticipated this trend. 'Pictures like *The Leopard Man* … and *Bedlam* …' he observes, 'feature women protagonists taking on monstrous male authority figures and, by proxy, patriarchy itself.'[11] Tom Weaver has long taken a similar view, stating that *Bedlam* is the 'first horror film to feature a feminist heroine'.[12]

Perhaps the most intriguing analysis of the influence the early Lewton films exerted upon 1940s cinema can be found in Snelson's *Phantom Ladies*. In a challenging examination of the way female audiences helped to shape the wartime horror genre, he identifies and traces the 'female monster cycle' of films that followed in the wake of *Cat People* and *I Walked with a Zombie*. 'Val Lewton's RKO production unit', he states, 'evolved a new type of female-centred horror film that would become the model for an industry-wide cycle'. He also states:

> Character types and themes from the female monster films were resultantly incorporated into popular film franchises and overlapping cycles, such as the "female mystery drama" and "psychiatric pictures" – critical categories that have now been subsumed into overarching categories of film noir and the women's film in feminist film scholarship and genre histories.[13]

Snelson examines numerous films across a range of genres in support of his thesis, including many not discussed in this chapter, such as *Son of Dracula* (1943), *The Spider Woman* (1943), *Jungle Woman* (1944), *Weird Woman* (1944) and *Phantom Lady* (1944). Whilst, arguably, he applies the definition of 'female monster' a little too broadly in some cases, the book is essential reading and invites further research on the subject.

Of the various low-budget films that sought to cash in on Lewton's 'formula' in the wake of his successes, perhaps the most shameless was Columbia's double-bill, *Cry of the Werewolf* and *Soul of a Monster* (1944). Each was written or co-written by a Lewton alumnus – respectively, Charles O'Neal and Edward Dein – and, as Snelson notes, each features a one man/two women triangle, plus a female 'monster'. *Cry of the Werewolf*, clearly emulating *Cat People*, focuses on a troubled woman of European descent who must forsake love to avoid being transformed into a murderous creature. Similarly, *Soul of a Monster*, about a man who is magically kept alive beyond his allotted lifespan though he is, in fact, dead, carries echoes of *Zombie*. Its press campaign even featured a zombie-like figure and taglines such as '[s]he was married to a walking dead man!' and '[s]he scratched his arm ... there was no blood!'[14]

One of the most successful appropriations of Lewton's formula can be seen in Republic's *The Woman Who Came Back* (1945), featuring a female protagonist, Lorna Webster (Nancy Kelly), who may or may not be possessed by the soul of a witch. As Lewton biographer Bansak states, the film 'should be recognised as a sincere effort by one of the few directors [Walter Colmes] who appeared to have some genuine understanding of the Lewton style'.[15] Elsewhere, Lewton's preference for female protagonists was echoed in Columbia's *The Return of the Vampire* (1943), which featured Frieda Inescourt as a female Van Helsing-type, pitted against Bela Lugosi's vampire.

At the other end of the budget scale, Lewton's influence is frequently cited in relation to *The Uninvited* (1944), Paramount's supernatural thriller based on Dorothy Macardle's best-selling novel *Uneasy Freehold*. It's interesting to note that both the novel and the film carry echoes of *Rebecca*, which is also referenced prominently in *The Uninvited*'s press book. An examination of the development timeline indicates that the purchase of the novel – and the initial, problematic stages of development – pre-dated the release of *Cat People*, though the later stages of script development and production could have been influenced by Lewton's early releases. Lewton stalwart Elizabeth Russell, who'd made a scene-stealing cameo in *Cat People*, appeared as the ghost of Mary Meredith (along with another actor from Lewton's film, Alan Napier) and the question of whether or not to show the ghost was the subject of much debate during production and post-production, evidence that Lewton's less-is-more approach was at least taken into consideration.[16]

Meanwhile, RKO had not yet finished with *Zombie*. In 1944 they purchased a story from MGM titled *Zombies on Broadway* and retasked it as a vehicle for Wally Brown and Alan Carney, the studio's answer to Abbott & Costello.[17] In the process, it was also transformed into a parody of *I Walked with a Zombie* – bypassing Lewton, who was probably horrified by the concept. *Zombies on Broadway* tells the story of two New

York press agents who travel to the island of San [sic] Sebastian in search of a genuine zombie to use as a promotional gimmick for a new nightclub. There, they encounter both Sir Lancelot and Darby Jones, playing roles similar to those found in the Lewton film. Bela Lugosi (who would appear in Lewton's *The Body Snatcher* soon afterwards) was also added to the mix.

The contrast between the two films – especially the cavalier presentation of its black actors – could not be more pronounced. The film singularly fails to respect the source material in the way a similar parody such as *Abbott & Costello Meet Frankenstein* (1948) managed a few years later. One suspects that Sir Lancelot belatedly realised he was being misused, given the half-hearted attempt to rework his 'Shame and Sorrow' calypso to suit the new material. Similarly, Darby Jones merely goes through the motions, and even Maurice Seiderman's zombie make-up utterly fails to recapture the look that Jones had sported in the original film. The reviews were decidedly mixed and the film performed poorly at the box office, failing even to recoup its costs for the studio.

BEYOND THE 1940s

Lewton's influence on the genre continued through the 1950s and 1960s, and beyond. *Cult of the Cobra* (1955) lifted elements of *Cat People*, whilst *Cat Girl* (1957) relied even more heavily on Lewton's film. Both Jacques Tourneur and Robert Wise paid homage to Lewton with *Night of the Demon* (1957) and *The Haunting* (1963) respectively. Writer Richard Matheson, an admirer of Lewton who had corresponded with him during his youth, joined with Charles Beaumont to adapt Fritz Leiber's *Conjure Wife* for the screen (for the second time, following Universal's *Weird Woman*, mentioned earlier). The result was the Lewtonesque *Night of the Eagle* (1962), directed by Sidney Hayers. Cult director Curtis Harrington was also heavily indebted to Lewton, and the influence is particularly evident in *Night Tide* (1961) and *The Cat Creature* (1973). During the 1960s, Hammer developed its own brand of female monsters, showcased in *The Gorgon* (1964) and *The Reptile* (1966).

The 'slasher' cycle of horror films, which exploded during the 1970s, had been startlingly anticipated by Lewton's *The Leopard Man* in 1943 – an observation explored by authors

Scott Preston and Peter Marra[18] – although the films it influenced often lacked the character development and genuine empathy for the victims that made *The Leopard Man* so singular. Similarly, the female horror protagonist pioneered by Lewton has since become the norm in the genre, though the debate continues as to whether later applications of this trend are feminist or misogynist. Meanwhile, the Lewon 'bus' – now known as the 'jump scare' – has become ubiquitous in contemporary horror films, often replacing any meaningful attempt to generate atmosphere and suspense. Lewton's less-is-more approach largely fell out of favour in the later decades of the twentieth century, by which time graphic horror had become the norm. More recently, however, occasional traces of his approach can still be detected, in stylish and intelligent films such as *The Others* (2001) and *Under the Shadow* (2016). Worthy of particular note is Pedro Costa's *Casa de Lava* (1995), which was heavily influenced by *Zombie* and used the film as its 'central source' during development.[19]

In the field of literature, Manuel Puig's acclaimed novel *Kiss of the Spider Woman* devotes an entire chapter to a retelling of *Cat People*, with further chapters inspired, at least partly, by *I Walked with a Zombie*. Similarly, parallels have been drawn between *Zombie* and Jean Rhys's 1966 prequel to *Jane Eyre*, *Wide Sargasso Sea*. Whilst many authors have noted that *Zombie* anticipated the novel by two decades, academic Judie Newman specifically identifies several narrative and thematic cross-overs – evidence which 'strongly suggests that Rhys had seen *I Walked with a Zombie*'.[20]

The turn of the century also brought a misguided remake of *Zombie*. A potential remake had been mooted as early as 1982 after producer Wilbur Stark (the 'executive consultant' on Paul Schrader's remake of *Cat People*) purchased the rights to remake a score of classic RKO properties.[21] Further trade press announcements followed in 1986, 1989 and 1998, each involving a different production company. The eventual film, *Ritual* (2002), directed by Ari Nesher, boasts a list of top names amongst its executive producers, including Richard Donner, Joel Silver, Robert Zemeckis and Walter Hill, though it's hard to equate their involvement with the end result, which bears only the most fleeting resemblance to *I Walked with a Zombie*. A measure of the gulf that separates the two films is the fact that the events in *Ritual* turn out to be part of a fraudulent real estate scheme.

IN CONCLUSION

The singular qualities of *I Walked with a Zombie* were recognised by the Library of Congress in September 1944. The picture was included on a list of '48 features ... released by film companies during the past year which are to be preserved for a permanent record by the library'.[22] The films had been selected by a special reviewing committee of the Museum of Modern Art Film Library which had been compelled, owing to a lack of storage space, to adopt a 'highly selective, rather than an inclusive acquisition policy'. Films were chosen that 'best record[ed], in one way or another, the life and tastes and preferences of the American people during the period in question', and which met one or more of a range of criteria, including 'those that indicate new trends or deviate in the substance or technique of motion picture production'.[23]

Discussing the selections for that year, Museum of Modern Art committee member Barbara Deming cited *Zombie* as an example of a cinematic, 'multivocal' art form, able to 'speak at several different levels simultaneously'. She noted that actors, when performing, 'involuntarily scuff in onto the carpet with them a bit of ... real life ... speak[ing] not for the play merely but for themselves', and that it is 'chiefly the realities of social antipathy that are likely to flare through the fabric of film – antipathies between race and race or class and class'. Singling out Lewton's film, she continued:

> Very occasionally the script will intentionally allow the actor to speak his natural piece. Thus in 'I Walked With A Zombie', produced by Val Lewton, the double-edged relationship between Negro and white is part of the film's original design. The film itself is sharply eloquent about the relationship because the Negro actors know so well what the play is they are playing; but it took a rare degree of sophistication on the part of Lewton to allow the actors this play.[24]

The representations of black people on screen continued to move one step backwards for every two forward steps taken, yet *Zombie* is recognised as one of the movies that 'emitted little organic wisps of new racial meanings' during that difficult time.[25] As noted by Gwenda Young, referencing the films of Spike Lee, '*Zombie*'s subversion of white discourse ... anticipate[d] new black cinema forty years later'.[26]

I Walked with a Zombie could not have been made – at least, not in the same way – had *Cat People* not preceded it. The two are inextricably linked – one, the culmination of a cinematic experiment that had begun with the other – and both are key defining texts in Lewton's *oeuvre*. Although Lewton's most personal films are arguably *The Seventh Victim* and *Curse of the Cat People*, *Zombie* is perhaps his most poetic and most beautiful. Tourneur stated that it was 'the best film I've ever done in my life'.[27] It was Ruth Lewton's favourite of all the films made by her husband. Siegel called it Lewton's 'most finished, most haunting film'.[28]

Despite *Zombie*'s critical and commercial impact, and its influence on the rich tapestry of genres that were brewing during the early 1940s, the film itself stands alone. Whilst numerous variations of *Cat People* were turned out by rivals and admirers alike, *Zombie* somehow proved impossible to emulate. Nothing quite like it has been seen since.

It is truly unique.

NOTES

1. Joel E. Siegel, *Val Lewton: The Reality of Terror* (Secker & Warburg, 1972), 128.
2. Robin Wood, *Hollywood from Vietnam to Reagan* (Columbia University Press, 2003), 77.
3. Carlos Clarens, *Horror Movies: An Illustrated Survey* (Secker & Warburg, 1967), 137.
4. John Brosnan, *The Horror People* (St Martin's Press, 1976), 73.
5. David Bordwell, *Reinventing Hollywood: How 1940s Filmmakers Changed Movie Storytelling* (University of Chicago Press, 2017), 16.
6. Alain Silver and James Ursini (eds), *Film Noir Reader 4* (Hal Leonard Corporation, 2004), 192.
7. Quoted in Mario DeGiglio-Bellemere, Charlie Ellbé and Kristopher Woofter (eds), *Recovering 1940s Horror Cinema: Traces of a Lost Decade* (Lexington Books, 2015), 5.
8. Edmund G. Bansak, *Fearing the Dark: The Val Lewton Career* (McFarland, 2003), 118.
9. Quoted in Silver and Ursini, *Film noir reader 4*, 192.
10. Helen Hanson, *Hollywood Heroines: Women in Film Noir and the Female Gothic Film* (I. B. Tauris, 2007), 225–226.
11. Ian Olney, 47–66, in DeGiglio-Bellemere, Ellbé and Woofter, *Recovering 1940s Horror Cinema*, 61.
12. Tom Weaver commentary, *Bedlam* (Warner, 2005) DVD.
13. Tim Snelson, *Phantom Ladies: Hollywood Horror and the Home Front* (Rutgers University Press, 2014), 2, 8.

14. *Cry of the Werewolf/Soul of a Monster* press book.
15. Bansak, *Fearing the Dark*, 382.
16. Clive Dawson, 'The Uninvited Revisited', *The Dark Side* 200, April 2019.
17. Bryan Senn, *Drums of Terror: Voodoo in the Cinema* (Midnight Marquee Press, 1998), 73.
18. See Scott Preston, 'The Strange Pleasure of The Leopard Man', *Cineaction* 71 (2007), 14–21, and Peter Marra in DeGiglio-Bellemere, Ellbé and Woofter, *Recovering 1940s Horror Cinema*, 27–45.
19. Nuno Baradas Jorge, 'Pedro Costa on the Island of the Dead', *Adaptation* 7/3 (2014), 253–264.
20. Judie Newman, *The Ballistic Bard: Postcolonial Fictions* (St Martin's Press, 1995), 18.
21. *Los Angeles Times*, 22 August 1982.
22. *Motion Picture Herald*, 30 September 1944, 34.
23. *Cleveland Plain Dealer*, 24 September 1944.
24. Barbara Deming, 'The Library of Congress Film Project', *Library of Congress Quarterly Journal of Current Acquisitions* 2/1 (1944), 10–11.
25. Thomas Cripps, *Making Movies Black: The Hollywood Message Movie from World War II to the Civil Rights Era* (Oxford University Press, 1993), 94.
26. Gwenda Young, 'The Cinema of Difference: Jacques Tourneur, Race and I Walked with a Zombie (1943)', *Irish Journal of American Studies* 7 (1998), 116.
27. Charles Higham and Joel Greenberg, *The Celluloid Muse: Hollywood Directors Speak* (New American Library, 1969), 248.
28. Siegel, *Val Lewton*, 41.

Bibliography

Agee, James. *Agee on Film*. Modern Library New York, 2000.

Bansak, Edmund G. *Fearing the Dark: The Val Lewton Career*. McFarland, 2003.

Bishop, Kyle William. *American Zombie Gothic: The Rise and Fall (and Rise) of the Walking Dead in Popular Culture*. McFarland, 2010.

Bodeen, DeWitt. *More from Hollywood!* A. S. Barnes, 1977.

Bordwell, David. *Reinventing Hollywood: How 1940s Filmmakers Changed Movie Storytelling*. University of Chicago Press, 2017.

Brosnan, John. *The Horror People*. St Martin's Press, 1976.

Clarens, Carlos. *Horror Movies: An Illustrated Survey*. Secker & Warburg, 1967.

Cripps, Thomas. *Making Movies Black: The Hollywood Message Movie from World War II to the Civil Rights Era*. Oxford University Press, 1993.

Dawson, Clive. 'The Uninvited Revisited.' *The Dark Side* 200 (2019).

DeGiglio-Bellemere, Mario, Charlie Ellbé and Kristopher Woofter, eds. *Recovering 1940s Horror Cinema: Traces of a Lost Decade*. Lexington Books, 2015.

Deming, Barbara. 'The Library of Congress Film Project.' *Library of Congress Quarterly Journal of Current Acquisitions* 2/1 (1944): 10–11.

Ellis, Sarah Reichardt and Michael Lee. 'Monsters, Meaning, and the Music of Chopin in American Horror Cinema of the 1930s and '40s.' *Journal of Musicological Research* 39/1 (2020): 24–41.

Fujiwara, Chris. *Jacques Tourneur: The Cinema of Nightfall*. McFarland, 2011.

Haining, Peter, ed. *Zombie: Stories of the Walking Dead*. Target Books, 1985.

Hanson, Helen. *Hollywood Heroines: Women in Film Noir and the Female Gothic Film*. I. B. Tauris, 2007.

Higham, Charles and Joel Greenberg. *The Celluloid Muse: Hollywood Directors Speak*. New American Library, 1969.

Jewell, Richard B. 'A History of RKO Radio Pictures, Incorporated, 1928–1942.' PhD thesis, University of Southern California, 1978.

Jewell, Richard B. 'RKO Film Grosses, 1929–1951: The C. J. Tevlin Ledger.' *Historical Journal of Film, Radio and Television* 14/1 (1994): 37–49.

Jewell, Richard B. *RKO Radio Pictures: A Titan is Born*. University of California Press, 2012.

Johnston, Clare and Paul Willemen. *Jacques Tourneur*. Edinburgh Film Festival, 1975.

Jorge, Nuno Baradas. 'Pedro Costa on the Island of the Dead.' *Adaptation* 7/3 (2014): 253–264.

Koppes, Clayton R. and Gregory D. Black. *Hollywood Goes to War: How Politics, Profits and Propaganda Shaped World War II Movies*. University of California Press, 1990.

Lauretis, Teresa de. 'I Walked with a Zombie: Colonialism and Intertextuality.' *EUtopias* 21 (2021): 23–35.

Lee, Michael. 'Sound and Uncertainty in the Horror Films of the Lewton Unit', in James Wierzbicki (ed.), *Music, Sound and Filmmakers*. Taylor & Francis, 2012, 107–121.

Lee, Michael. *Music in the Horror Films of Val Lewton*. Edinburgh University Press, 2022.

Leff, Leonard J. *Hitchcock and Selznick*. University of California Press, 1987.

MacQueen, Scott. Booklet for *Roy Webb: Music for the Films of Val Lewton*. Marco Polo, 2000. CD.

Mank, Gregory William. *It's Alive! The Classic Cinema Saga of Frankenstein*. Tantivy Press, 1981.

Mank, Gregory William, Philip Riley and George Turner. *The Wolf Man*. MagicImage Filmbooks, 1993.

Nemerov, Alexander. *Icons of Grief: Val Lewton's Home Front Pictures*. University of California Press, 2005.

Newman, Judie. *The Ballistic Bard: Postcolonial Fictions*. St Martin's Press, 1995.

Newman, Kim. *Cat People*. BFI Film Classics, 1999.

Nochimson, Martha P. 'Val Lewton at RKO: The Social Dimensions of Horror.' *Cineaste* 31/4 (2006): 9–17.

Nowell, Richard, ed. *Merchants of Menace: The Business of Horror Cinema*. Bloomsbury, 2014.

O'Brien, Geoffrey. 'Artisan of the Unseen.' *Film Comment* 38/4 (2002): 46–49.

Ohmer, Susan. *George Gallup in Hollywood*. Columbia University Press, 2006.

Peary, Dannis. 'Mark Robson Remembers RKO, Welles & Val Lewton.' *Velvet Light Trap* 10 (1973): 32–37.

Preston, Scott. 'The Strange Pleasure of The Leopard Man.' *Cineaction* 71 (2007): 14–21.

Price, Michael H. *Forgotten Horrors, Volume 10: The Missing Years*. Cremo Studios, 2016.

Schatz, Thomas. *The Genius of the System: Hollywood Filmmaking in the Studio Era*. Pantheon Books, 1998.

Seabrook, W. B. *The Magic Island*. Literary Guild of America, 1929.

Senn, Bryan. *Drums of Terror: Voodoo in the Cinema*. Midnight Marquee Press, 1998.

Server, Lee. *Screenwriter: Words Become Pictures*. Main Street Press, 1987.

Siegel, Joel E. *Val Lewton: The Reality of Terror*. Secker & Warburg, 1972.

Siegel, Joel E. 'Tourneur Remembers.' *Cinefantastique* 2/4 (1973): 24–25.

Silver, Alain and James Ursini, eds. *Film Noir Reader 4*. Hal Leonard Corporation, 2004.

Siodmak, Curt. *Wolf Man's Maker: Memoir of a Hollywood Writer*. Scarecrow Press, 2001.

Snelson, Tim. *Phantom Ladies: Hollywood Horror and the Home Front*. Rutgers University Press, 2014.

Stewart, Catherine A. *Long Past Slavery: Representing Race in the Federal Writers' Project*. University of North Carolina Press, 2016.

Telotte, J. P. *Dreams of Darkness: Fantasy and the Films of Val Lewton*. University of Illinois Press, 1985.

Tourneur, Jacques. 'Taste without Clichés.' *Films and Filming* 12/2 (1965): 9–11.

Turner, George. 'Val Lewton's Cat People.' *Cinefantastique* 12/4 (1982): 23–27.

Walsh, Meaghan. 'Survivors and Victims: Gothic Feminism, Deconstruction and Colonialism in I Walked with a Zombie.' Masters dissertation, Savannah College Art and Design, 2008.

Weaver, Tom. *Return of the B Science Fiction and Horror Heroes: The Mutant Melding of Two Volumes of Classic Interviews*. McFarland, 2000.

Wood, Robin. 'The Shadow Worlds of Jacques Tourneur.' *Film Comment* 8/2 (1972): 64–70.

Wood, Robin. 'Notes for a Reading of I Walked with a Zombie.' *Cine Action* 3/4 (1986): 6–20.

Wood, Robin. *Hollywood from Vietnam to Reagan*. Columbia University Press, 2003.

Young, Gwenda. 'The Cinema of Difference: Jacques Tourneur, Race and I Walked with a Zombie (1943).' *Irish Journal of American Studies* 7 (1998): 101–119.

Printed and bound by CPI Group (UK) Ltd, Croydon, CR0 4YY
17/09/2024

14558354-0001